JOURNEY TO
JERUSALEM

JOURNEY TO
JERUSALEM

RE-VISITING BIBLICAL FAITH
IN THE COUNTRY OF ITS ORGIN

Written by Trevor Pitt
Illustrated by Linda Birch

BOOKS

Copyright (c) 2001 O Books
Text © 2001 Trevor Pitt
Illustrations © 2001 Linda Birch

ISBN 1 903816 01 7

Designed by
ANDREW MILNE DESIGN

Write to:
JOHN HUNT PUBLISHING LTD
46A West Street, Alresford, Hampshire SO24 9AU, UK

The rights of Trevor Pitt as author of this work and Linda Birch as illustrator have been asserted
in accordance with the Copyright, Designs and Patents Act 1988.

A CIP catalogue record for this book is available from the British Library.

Printed in Malaysia

Visit our website at: o-books.net

Contents

A Foreword by
the Archbishop of York

AT ONCE INFORMATIVE AND MEDITATIVE, THOUGHTFUL AND THOUGHT-PROVOKING, THIS IS ABOVE ALL AN AGREEABLE, READABLE BOOK. IT IS JUST THE SORT OF BOOK WHICH ANY PILGRIM TO THE HOLY LAND WILL BE GLAD TO HAVE — BEFORE, DURING AND AFTER THEIR PILGRIMAGE.

BEFORE, IT WILL ENLIVEN ANTICIPATION OF THE RICH POSSIBILITIES OF EXPERIENCE WHICH LIE AHEAD. DURING, IT CAN BE USED TO CHECK FACTS AND — MORE IMPORTANTLY — TO COMPARE THE RESONANCE OF SHARED EXPERIENCE. AFTER, IT WILL HELP CONSOLIDATE AND FOCUS THAT EXPERIENCE, GIVING IT THE SORT OF FORM AND CUTTING EDGE WHICH TRANSFORMS IT INTO A TRULY SPIRITUAL TOOL: A TOOL WHICH WILL REFINE THEIR UNDERSTANDING OF THE LORD IN WHOSE FOOTSTEPS THEY HAVE WALKED AND IN WHOSE COMPANY THEY TRAVEL STILL.

THE READER CAN ONLY BE DEEPLY INDEBTED TO TREVOR AND LINDA, WHO HAVE INVESTED SO FULLY OF THEMSELVES, OF THEIR FAITH AND THEIR LOVE OF OUR LORD'S OWN LAND.

DAVID EBOR

Introduction to the illustrations

I didn't want to go — to begin with. Invited to accompany my husband on a study course to the Holy Land in 1995, and being an illustrator and painter, I determined not to waste time during the visit, so packed some paints and a sketchbook. One sketchbook was soon filled and I had to buy another. The place completely captivated me and I could not stop drawing. Working at every opportunity, I managed to draw and paint even from the back of the bus as it bounced along uneven terrain and desert roads.

The pictures in this book are glimpses of what any visitor might see. Time would not permit me more than that — but this book is a visual diary of the places we travelled through. The things I could not record were the smells! They are acute memory enhancers. Sometimes, looking through the sketchbooks is enough to evoke that curious mixture of smells — garbage, sweet spices and raw meat. Not pleasant, but odours that would have been common in the first century so one is smelling history.

It was fascinating to observe the way people reacted to the places they were visiting, especially the venerated sites. Flocks of faithful from all nations congregate there, obediently following their guides. One party even wore yellow baseball caps to identify them, so they resembled chicks chasing a mother hen!

British postbox near Jaffa Gate

Away from the well-known towns and cities the landscape communicated a sort of odd familiarity — the wilderness and desolation sublime yet somehow known. Sleepless in the desert, the most awesome dawn that followed was worth the long waking night.

I have tried to record my impressions of a troubled region and those who visit it — but I think first century people would have little difficulty recognising the place as it exists today — not much has really changed.

Linda Barnh

Introduction

his book is born from the experience of several study visits and field trips I have
made to the "Holy Land", that is, all the biblical lands of the ancient near middle
east, stretching today from Egypt to Syria. From the time when I first took a sab-
batical period of study in Jerusalem in 1988, I have been in love with the place, infuriat-
ing though it often is. In recent years I have arranged field trips in biblical studies for ministerial students. I believe that we best study the biblical text in its primary context. The
journey recounted in these pages was one such visit in search of that original setting.

I am not an expert in Middle Eastern affairs. I have little first-hand knowledge of the
language and cultures of the region beyond what I have picked up on my travels. Nor am
I a specialist in the worlds of classical antiquity. I am a theological educator and a Christian
priest in the Anglican tradition. I am also Principal of the North East Oecumenical Course
(known as NEOC), a training course for ministerial students in the north east of England.
I have tried to share with them something of my own enthusiasm for Holy Land studies,
and to enable them to make the theological discoveries that the place affords.

I am aware of the dangers. The state of Israel welcomes a million tourists each year, and
for many of them it is just another Mediterranean destination: sun, sand and antiquities,
with biblical associations thrown in. It is perfectly possible for visitors to remain immune
to the contemporary reality of the lives of those who live there. This is particularly true
of those on package tours, visiting religious sites and shrines yet paying scant regard to the
struggles of actual Christian communities. I have never organised or led a Christian tour
or pilgrimage to the Holy Land. Pilgrimages and field trips cater for different interests, as
I hope may become clear in what follows. This does not mean that students and teachers
of the Bible are not also pilgrims.

NEOC has been arranging Summer Schools for its students in the Holy Land since
1995. This took some doing! Not because the travel, the terrain, the climate or the terrorism are particularly difficult (though that is certainly true). The main obstacles were

Above: Jerusalem, the paradoxical, puzzling and challenging focus of our theological and historical journey.

people who believed that the Holy Land is a place only for tourists and not for serious theologians. My mission soon became a determined effort to prove them wrong, and our study visits have been designed as essential and integral parts of the theological education we provide for ministerial students. Their first purpose is to make it possible to read the biblical texts in the actual place of their production so that their interpretation comes alive in fresh, and often unexpected, ways. It helps us all to enjoy the Bible, and become more intimately familiar with it. Secondly, and perhaps even more importantly, *reading the Bible with our feet* (and not just as a literary text) allows us to be more patient with its meanings. We abuse the Bible if we treat it only as a source of simple messages for today's issues or proof texts to back up our own fixed opinions. Trying to see the land of the Bible as the kind of place it really is, a small territory of seething hatreds and bitter divisions, belonging to and sacred to the three major faiths of the Abrahamic tradition, helps us all understand more deeply the multi-faith world in which our lives and ministries are set. Learning for ministry has its basic setting in the student's reflection on actual experience, because the church's ministry cannot be remote from secular realities, from the needs of people and their actual situations.

MORE THAN HEAD KNOWLEDGE

The experience of learning together in the biblical lands is always more than the study of an academic subject, and serves to emphasise that doing theology is not merely book learning. Knowledge of God, true theology, is found in personal experience, relationships between people and in the everyday life of communities. The intention of all our Holy Land visits is to infect theological students with an enthusiasm for learning in these ways, ways that are open to everyone, not merely to the especially religious.

My wife Linda first joined me on a visit to the Holy Land in 1995. She is a professional artist and illustrator, and at once found inspiration in the light and the subjects, the landscapes, the people and the places. She has accompanied me on visits ever since, trying to capture the special appeal of the place in her chosen medium, watercolour. Many of her paintings are reproduced here, and you may judge whether the text accompanies the artwork, or vice versa. We have together experienced the place and the people, and eventually decided to put our separate interests, the artistic and the theological, together in a way that we hope is complementary.

For most of our visits, our hosts have been the community of St. George's College, an ecumenical study centre located in the compound of the Anglican Cathedral in east Jerusalem. Most of my own learning, and the opportunities for study, have been the result of the varied and stimulating courses run by the college and its staff. In particular, I would record an immense debt of gratitude and affection to Henry Carse, Director of Special Programmes, who has been a source of continual inspiration and encouragement. In his company many ideas in this book began to take root. I would also like to place on record my thanks to former NEOC students who have accompanied me on several field trips in the Holy Land, and who have undoubtedly suffered as well as benefited from my enthusiasms. Only they will know how much they have contributed, and for their contribution to these pages I am truly grateful.

PILGRIMAGE

A journey to the Holy Land is more than a visit to an interesting place. Many people who make the journey call it a "pilgrimage" and want it to be a "journey of a lifetime." A pilgrimage, by means of a physical journey, is an attempt to refocus "the Way", the apt description of Christian practice given in its earliest literature (Acts 9:1, 22:4).

Every life is a journey. A person's coming to faith in God through Jesus Christ is itself a journey. Not a single, isolated decision, or a one-off commitment of an individual to God, but a process, a lifelong exploration of learning, growth and conviction. Nor is it ever an unaccompanied journey. "Journeying" is one of the most frequently recurring biblical themes. This is perhaps hardly surprising, but it is also worth

Right: A map of the Holy Land, showing some of the places of significance on our route.

bearing in mind that "pilgrim" is a word nowhere found in the New Testament. "Tourist" likewise! The basic narrative structure of the Gospels is the journey of Jesus himself towards Jerusalem. It is both a theological and a literal journey. A pilgrimage, a literal journey, is not a requirement of the Christian faith, as Muslims journey to Mecca, or as Jews long to be "next year in Jerusalem." A Christian is not preoccupied with holy places, only with a concern to make the whole world a holy place.

Yet for Christians who seek to orient their lives towards a goal, the image of journey remains a powerful one. The biblical tradition frequently likens Christians to strangers in an alien environment, pilgrims on the way to a true homeland, while still being commit-

Above: The traveller in a foreign land; what do host and guest see in each other?

ted to the world in which they live, and to the communities of people of which they are part. Some element of ambiguity is therefore essential to Christian understanding, and to all journeys they undertake. One early Christian writer, Diognetus, expressed this paradox when he said that "every foreign land is their fatherland and every fatherland a foreign land."

Attention to the biblical sources reveals this clearly. Abraham was perhaps more a migrant than a pilgrim, and the New Testament echoes the theme of "sojourning" - "here we have no abiding city" (Hebrews 13:14). Moses led his people on an exodus (literally "a way out") but was not allowed to settle in the promised land. Those who did eventually settle were not successful and spent long years in exile from the land in which, later, even the Son of Man was to have "nowhere to lay his head". Exodus, exile and settlement are profound themes that continue to scar the lives of all who live in the Holy Land. Those who journey there from the West today cannot ignore the contemporary dimension of these age-old themes, or the footsteps of those Christians who went before them.

CHRISTIAN ATTITUDES

Historically, Christian attitudes to pilgrimage changed when the Emperor Constantine began his building projects in the Holy Land. The tragic results of that misplaced practice of giving religious significance to particular sites have been the Christian Crusades, commercial tourism, the partition of Palestine and Western efforts to internationalise Jerusalem. People have flocked to the sites in increasing numbers since they were first opened up to Western exploration in the nineteenth century. Of course, such visits never have, and never can, take place in a political vacuum. As the Ottoman Empire began to crumble through the nineteenth century, so the international struggle for global power and influence focused on this strategic land bridge between west and east. At first, such journeys were far from easy and comforts were few, but the sense of adventure drew the curious and the committed along with the diplomats and the businessmen. Their travels were recorded and published in sufficient numbers (and with sufficient dross) to deter further attempts. Yet they continue to be made!

In the nineteenth century Thomas Cook brought thousands of visitors on "Biblical, Educational and General Tours", which must have been exotic and intense experiences for those who could afford and endure them. Like many who come today, there must also have been disappointment. Herman Melville, in 1857, found the Church of the Holy Sepulchre nothing but a cheat, and the whole experience "an accumulation of stone … stony walls and stony fields, stony houses and stony tombs, stony eyes and stony hearts". Protestant visitors especially found little in the local Christian culture with which they could identify, and still today many "pilgrims" prefer to bring their own styles and understandings with them rather than encounter something genuinely different. Yet like Mark Twain before them (not the most devout pilgrim!), all need to find some way of coming

Right: *The camel tolerates today's tourist as it has countless masters since long before the time of Christ.*

Right: There is a tradition that the pomegranete has 99 seeds – each is a different name for Allah. The camel knows the 100th, hence it's expression.

to terms with what they find when they are "actually in the illustrious old city where Solomon dwelt, where Abraham held converse with the Deity, and where walls still stand that witnessed the spectacle of the Crucifixion".

This same desire to be moved and challenged and inspired by "the very place" is as old as the first Christian pilgrimages in the fourth century. In the nineteenth century this desire was famously and exquisitely expressed in the beautiful watercolours of David Roberts. Despite their lack of authenticity, his paintings belong with the long search for things that go beyond actuality, beyond what can be experienced with the senses. Yet a challenge remains. Amid the squalor and corruption and violence that are the legacy of the centuries, how is it possible at least to glimpse holiness in the so-called "holy places"? To find heaven in the ordinary?

BENEFITS

Many Christians have no desire to visit the Holy Land at all, and see only sordid commercialism, tourism masquerading as spirituality, and theological naivety. They imagine that such visits are only a futile search for the earthly historical Jesus - futile, because so overlaid with centuries of cultural and pious clutter. Most Christians find a living Jesus in the realities of their own lives, their churches and communities, their experience and commitments, and in the people around them every day. Jesus is not to be looked for in one place, but in every place, because if he is not in my place, then he is not in any place. Yet this approach all too easily becomes complacency, because a journey to another place puts what is familiar and secure at risk. No-one goes on this kind of journey, however, looking for something they have not already found. That is why it is always more than sightseeing, and a good deal more surprising and disturbing.

As one student put it, asked to define what he was doing in joining this study visit:

To gain insight into the context when Jesus lived there.

To experience the context when we are there.

To explore our own context more deeply on returning home.

This is the ambition of this book.

Right: Patience is a virtue. Everything's going to be alright ... isn't it?

Chapter One

THE JOURNEY — OUTWARDS

Most flights from the UK seem to arrive at Ben Gurion airport, Tel Aviv, around midnight. The first time I landed here, about ten years before, I remember being shocked and not a little frightened, queuing for passport control and passing slowly in front of a memorial listing the names of passengers who had just happened to be wrong place at the wrong time, gunned down by terrorists in that same arrivals hall some years earlier. The severe interrogation had been a sharp reminder of the nature of my destination. The arrivals hall seems to have been rebuilt since that first visit, but memories of such atrocities linger long in this land of long memories. Tonight the queues were quicker, the interrogations less severe.

We successfully negotiated the arrival and immigration formalities and feeling pleased with ourselves fully expected our guide and lecturer to greet us in the arrivals hall. After half an hour of looking, checking, waiting, consulting the information desk, and pretending to the rest of the party that everything was OK, I began to wonder why I had embarked on this visit. Why had I come?

THE DESERT

Part of our journey was to include several days in the desert. I now felt I was already there - in a very real desert, not the one I had planned, with a guide. Just off the plane and straight into an alien environment, only just managing to convince the other members of the group that everything was perfectly in order, under control, just hang on. Remember this is the Middle East. A different time frame. It helps relieve the inevitable build-up of frustration ingrained in westerners to recall three important notions which tend to define the way life is experienced here - inshalah (if God is willing …), bukrah (well, perhaps tomorrow …), and malesh (it's not important anyway!).

"DOING THEOLOGY WITH THE FEET"

This journey had been long in the planning. My previous visits to the Holy Land had convinced me that going to the place itself, "doing theology with the feet", offered wonderfully fresh opportunities for biblical study and theological reflection. I had somehow persuaded both the students and the governing body of my ministerial training course that this visit was a viable prospect. I had spent the best part of two years arguing and explaining. People had eventually come to trust my intuition and invest in my vision. We had arrived. The last piece of luggage was removed from the carousel. Travellers melted into the night, taxis and buses disappeared, shops drew down their shutters and something approaching silence settled on the hall. I put out a public address call for our guide, our tour company, anything I could think of. I did one more check of the taxi stand, the coach bay, the approach road, and tried desperately to think of what Plan B might have been, had we felt we needed one. I had been here myself several times before, but could my limited knowledge get this group to our starting point, Beersheba? Suddenly, out of the night, apparently from nowhere, our guide materialised, all smiles, flashing greetings. Panic over for the moment. Sheer relief. Only at moments like these do we realise how much we trust others, how much we rely on our assumption that things will remain in place.

Our first lesson in acclimatisation over, we boarded our coach, which I'm sure hadn't been there a few minutes before. But it was reassuring and familiar. Expect to be surprised. Don't panic. We sped along empty highways south through Lod, Ramla, Rehovot, bypassing Ashdod and Ashkelon - the ancient land of the Philistines - to the Negev, the desert … and sleep soon overtook us. Two hours later, sometime after 3am, we drew in to the Desert Inn, Beersheba. Large, comfortable rooms, a welcoming bowl of fruit, a swimming pool promised for the morning, but sleep …

Left: 3am. Dog sleeping: hotel foyer Beersheba.

Chapter Two

A WELL IN THE DESERT

The swimming pool, like the whole hotel, guests and staff alike, is full of Russians, who now make up 20% of the Israeli population (a further 20% are Arabs - maybe part of the key to understanding the tensions here). The sun was already high in the sky, the heat intense, the light powerful, and every surface baked hard and dry. We did not stay long in this large, sprawling modern university city. Beershaba is the fourth largest in the state of Israel after Tel Aviv, Haifa and Jerusalem. In 1917 the Allied armies were here, having tried and failed to take Gaza from the Turks. They had then refocused their campaign on Jerusalem, taking Beersheba first on 31 October 1917. Only ten weeks later Jerusalem was taken by General Allenby. For British visitors, these facts were reminders of the vast changes the area has seen during the twentieth century. They also point to the associations that in so many ways connect British people in particular to such an ancient and formative place. (British policy in this region in the early twentieth century did much to create the modern Middle East with all its social and political fault lines).

We drove out of the city into the surrounding desert, the Negev, a word meaning "parched", which is certainly accurate. It occupies 60% of modern Israel - but so much more than territory is defined by desert. The biblical narratives themselves, for example, which we have come to explore (something tells me that this way of doing theology will be hard on the feet!). The biblical story of Israel begins in the desert - and in this one! The character of the desert can tell us so much about the faith born here from people's struggle with its stillness … The standard definition of aridity is less than 4" of rainfall per annum, and the Negev certainly qualifies. The desert is unforgiving, and dehydration sets in quickly. So our last stop was to buy bottles of water, gallons of it! We are exhorted to drink frequently, and never to be without an adequate supply of water. Just beyond the city limits, we stopped at a vantage point surmounted by an army memorial of 1948, like many in modern Israel, all done in a strange brutalist manner, blocks of angular concrete, fitting reminders of the recent past.

ABRAHAM

Farther away, a railway line leads away from a mineral extraction plant, making the air dusty and the horizon hazy. The famed Israeli enterprise of making the desert bloom is beginning to happen here. The stone is white limestone, topped with a wind-eroded fine dry dust that becomes fertile once crops are planted and irrigated. Appropriately enough, we noticed tamarisk trees growing here, and remembered their first planter, Abraham (Genesis 21:33). As we spent some time contemplating this scene, acclimatising ourselves to the fierce heat, it seemed a good moment to reflect on one of the "terrible" texts of the Abraham cycle, the rejection of Abraham's Egyptian wife Hagar and her son Ishmael (Genesis 21). Islam tells the alternative story of the offering of Ishmael, rather than that of Isaac, Sarah's son, in Genesis 22. In fact, both faiths, Judaism and Islam, now understand themselves as rejected by the other! These narratives have so much to tell. An

Below: The luxury of swimming at Beersheba, surrounded by the aridity of the Negev Desert.

embarrassment, perhaps, to many devout readers, but I think a truthful accompaniment on this stage of the journey, and an echo of so much similar suffering among the refugees of our own century. The desert has a strange and awesome beauty that should not blind us to its hostility and desolation. Banished by Abraham and Sarah into the desert, God provided what was necessary for Hagar, a well (and eventually a wife for Ishmael!). Water sources are matters of life and death here. Bedouin culture (and the Abraham saga offers many parallels with the traditional Bedouin way of life) is transmitted through physical symbols rather than abstract ideas. So Abraham's primary symbolic activity is his offering hospitality to three visitors who come to his tent for water - and for life.

Pausing at this spot, we began our bible study, not in the accustomed way by discussing the meaning of the texts, but by pouring the water of life over each other's hands, then spending fifteen minutes in silence. A fresh wind blew dust everywhere. A train of mineral wagons slowly drew out of a loading terminus heading north. We were at the very edge of the real desert, the high rise development of modern Beersheba providing a backdrop and an outpost. Our journey will take us deeper into what is known in Hebrew as

Below: Memorial to Israeli Desert Campaign, 1948.

shimmah, the desolation or despair of the desert, but meaning literally "What is there?" and pronounced with a stuttering sound. The very sound of the word seems to suggest the unclear, hazy horizon towards which we will be travelling. But we did not go far.

A short distance from the modern city lies the small site of *Tel Sheba* preserving the debris of successive ancient communities. It is initially surprising to find the level of older civilisations considerably higher than the present ground surface. This is because low buildings with shallow foundations could most easily be built on the rubble of previous structures - at least until the Byzantine period.

BEERSHEBA

Beersheba exists at the borders - ancient Israel was often understood to stretch "from Dan to Beersheba". Some hewn stones discovered here can be reconstructed into an Israelite horned altar, and a replica of the original is displayed in a shaded courtyard. This suggests a date earlier than 620 BC, when the Judean king Josiah centralised all sacrificial ritual in Jerusalem. The horns presumably had a utilitarian original function, designed to support containers, or to tie the sacrifice. In appearance, however, they seem to symbolise an animal (ayil, meaning ram, has a Hebrew root close to el, God). It is hard to imagine the sight and smell of an actual sacrifice in this quiet place. It was easier to visualise, as demonstrated by one of the group, a refugee or fugitive arriving at such a place and clinging to the horns of the altar for sanctuary. As she did so, her outstretched arms at once evoked another image of total vulnerability, and another place of sacrifice.

The concept of sacrifice is common to all religions, but repellent to modern thinking. In the story of the binding of Isaac, God appears to command, and Abraham appears willing to carry out, what is without rational or moral excuse. How can the taking of life be life-giving? This ancient horned altar holds a clue. The Latin root of our word sacrifice, *sacer/facere*, literally "making holy", has, in part at least, led to a damaging misunderstanding within Christianity. Sacrifice understood as "propitiation", people trying to placate or appease an angry God by offering him presents. No wonder Christianity is widely rejected! But the root (*corebh*) of the Hebrew word for sacrificial offering, *corban,* implies not separation from an angry God, but intimate closeness with a loving God. In Hebrew thinking, it is God who continually offers the sacrifice, the giving of himself, in creating the world. Our mistake was to conceive God as a Being who demands to receive sacrifice from us - precisely the wrong way round! Most world religions understand the creation as an activity of sacrificial self-giving by its Creator. For Christians, the image of the man stretched on a cross is the supreme expression of the lov-

Below: Shade and relief.

ing closeness and the costly self-giving, the sacrifice, of God, the Creator identified completely with the human being. Certainly most Jewish, Christian and Islamic re-tellings of the Isaac/Ishmael story find in it an example of voluntary self-sacrifice in relation to God and other people, a symbol of the true nature of religious commitment. In Christian tradition Isaac quickly became an anticipation of the sacrificial death of Jesus.

THE WELL

Outside the wall of the ancient city is a large well. Remembering the dispute between Abraham and Abimelech about the digging of a well (from which episode Beersheba gets its name), rather strangely recounted in Genesis 21, it is tempting to ask whether this stone structure is the well in question. But, as always, simple historical questions about the biblical narratives, "Is this it?", "Did it really happen like this?" do not go to the heart of what the Bible is saying. The sheer fact is that someone dug a well, and the person who first told this story knew of its existence. The date and precise location are hardly significant, but rather the impact of the story and the way it is told. It is about water - and that's the most important fact of all in the desert. There are two kinds of water sources. The diggers of wells and the builders of cisterns can claim to own them, whereas springs, on the other hand, belong to God. So Abraham's quarrel is about the ownership of the well that Abimelech's men had seized. Abraham offers seven lambs, not to prove that he dug the well, but to renegotiate the facts on the ground. In other words, history and storytelling overlap right from the start; there are no original, definite, incontrovertible facts to which appeal can be made. History must be reconstructed on the basis of narrative, and not the other way round. This remains the case, not merely throughout the Bible and our interpretation of it, but also within the disputed Holy Land today. Facts are not sufficient, because there are always counter-facts. Jews and Palestinians today have much the same problem, especially over water and land, as Abraham and Abimelech. They need to renegotiate history. In both cases, ancient and modern, there are issues of life and death at stake.

Moving further in, the ruins of the city gate complex display a layout common to ancient Israelite urban settlements. There was no right-angled arrangement with a benched passage here, as at other sites, but even so this was clearly not a simple opening in the wall, nor was its purpose simply for defence. Here are dis-

Below: Horned altar.

Above: Modern Beersheba.

played the foundations of rooms either side of the entrance where the judges or elders sat. They perfectly illustrate the meaning of the many passages in the Hebrew scriptures describing the dispensation of justice and the settlement of disputes at the city gate. Well within the walls of ancient cities stood the temple and the palace, the centres of priestly and royal power. Clearly what happened at the gate offered an alternative power structure, "closer to the people". It is significant that Abraham, and Rebecca, are both promised, among other things, that their descendants will possess their enemies' gates (Genesis 22:17, 24:60), presumably the symbol of real control.

In later years the gate became the focus of royal power, as kings sought perhaps to assert their sovereignty over the more traditional seats of power in the community. The prophet Samuel met Saul "in the gate" (1Samuel 9:18); David is found "sitting in the gate" of Mahanaim awaiting news of his son Absalom's rebellion in Jerusalem (2 Samuel 18:24). Later still, in the Persian period, archaeology reveals that governors' residences were often sited close to the gate. In Jerusalem, Pilate's residence is thought to have been where the Citadel now stands, at the Jaffa gate. The significance of the statement in Hebrews 13:12 is clear, that Jesus died outside the gate – an early Christian affirmation of the real nature of authority. But then, the Hebrew word for governor is moshel, cognate with mashal, meaning literally "one who tells parables". There is surprising power in stories. The figure of Jesus suddenly emerges with a new clarity, the man who taught with authority, in parables! We are getting more deeply involved as our journey begins to weave its way not only into the desert but also into the complex texture of the biblical story.

Returning to the hotel for a shower and a beer, we sat in the garden in the relatively cool air. We shared a meal with our driver, a Melchite Christian from Nazareth. All faiths, and all traditions, meet here in the Holy Land - or could meet, but more often encounter each other only in dispute, ignorance and misunderstanding. Western Christians are no better, bringing their own local customs and familiar liturgies rather than engaging with the differences! At least the food is different!

I was called upon to preside at a celebration of Eucharist - it was still Saturday by western reckoning, but the Jewish sabbath had already finished - the sky was full of stars. Christians also sometimes reckon days in the Jewish manner from sunset to sunset, and it was convenient for us to do so. I made some comment on a biblical passage set for the day, the famous hymn of Christ in Philippians 2:5-11. I explained briefly the conundrum at the heart of this text, because it serves as a pointer to the leading question of this journey. Who is and was Jesus of Nazareth? The text speaks of his "emptying", but of what? Are we to understand Christ as fully God, but who "emptied" himself of divinity in order to "reach down" completely to us? Or are we to understand Christ as fully human, and who "emptied" himself totally in order to offer completely the full and final sacrifice of himself? Can we find answers to these crucial questions by being here? Certainly Jesus Christ is part of a longer story, and today we started at the beginning.

THE CALL OF CREATION

The other set passage, Genesis 12:1-9, introduces the longer story with the "call" of Abraham by God. This surprising God has previously called the whole creation into being, so it follows that the call of creation, and the call of Abraham and his descendants, the general and the specific, the world and the church, are not separate calls, but are bound together in the long story of God. Abraham is a model of the true disciple. In his case, the call was to leave his own country and undertake a long journey. The journey is a metaphor for faith. It is also an actual journey through some of the places and sites we shall visit ourselves. Of course, the places mentioned in Abraham's story (Ai, Bethel, Shechem) were also Israelite shrines for those later writers and compilers of the text. This is also therefore a theological journey. Life and theology too, are bound together.

So what of Abraham's journey and its connection with our own? Abraham goes south towards the Negev in stages. His life of faith is a pursuit of land, and the *land* is a major biblical motif, not as a "holy land", but a "land of the Holy One". Abraham is in the land with all his possessions and dependants, but he never owns it; the Canaanites are also living here. The story is subversive of ideologies of settlement, ownership, and claims to possession. Even God is nomadic, without a fixed place.

So, Abraham is called to leave his own place, although he brought all his possessions and dependants with him! In our case, coming to this new place, we have tried to travel light, making great efforts to leave our Western cultural and religious baggage behind, to "empty ourselves" of Western assumptions, trying not to import and impose all our presuppositions and prejudices on what we see and hear in the East. We have to allow this journey into new and unfamiliar experiences to speak in all its strangeness. Not treating it as a chance simply to confirm what we already know or believe, we must see it as an opportunity to open ourselves up to what we do not yet know.

Right: Ancient well at the gate of Old Beersheba.

Above: Dawn in the Negev.

Chapter Three

WANDERING IN THE DESERT

Sunday morning. The alarm sounded at 3.15am. Two young T-shirted security people watched our coach departing into the night. After an hour's journey climbing into the Negev highlands, we began to walk into the hills, guided only by torches, waiting for dawn. It was still dark, and we had no idea where we were. It seemed amazingly still and cool as we climbed over rocky terrain to a small cairn where a biblical meditation was offered on the theme of rejection, not this time concerned with Abraham but with Moses, who after killing an Egyptian escaped to Midian. Today we were going to cross the desert on foot, and recall some episodes in the biblical narratives of the Exodus.

After an hour or so, we regrouped and waited in silence for sunrise. Colours changed and forms appeared imperceptibly. Just before the sun appeared over the horizon, it suddenly rose on a silver airship that appeared somewhat incongruously, I thought, sailing (it seems the right word) high above us. We heard no sound from any motor and it appeared to be moving crosswise rather than directly forwards. In fact it remained above us all day. What was it doing there? A survey, perhaps, or maybe security surveillance? If it had been looking for us, there would have been no escape.

Moses was forced to escape because, in seeking to achieve something worthwhile, he acted hastily, without reflection or wisdom. So often we want to be active, and cannot keep still. The desert enforces stillness upon us.

A high railway embankment ran across the wadi in front of us, the freight line from a large phosphate plant deep in the biblical wilderness of Zin (for that is where we were). The bank was too high and steep to climb without proper equipment, and seemed to sym-

Below: An airship keeps watch.

bolise the barriers we create both for ourselves and for others through lack of reflection and wisdom. A path, however, lay through a low narrow concrete tunnel constructed beneath the embankment. Slowly we walked through this tunnel, silently and bent very low. It was a "narrow place", the literal meaning of the Hebrew word for Egypt, *mitzrayim*. The Talmud relates how the Hebrews were forced to make bricks in pits of mud. Pregnant women were not allowed to stop their work, not even when their babies were born, which of course then fell into the mud. It was the Hebrew's own flesh and blood that built the cities of their oppressors. Our little experience of a way through a barrier served to remind us of the many ways in which human beings are oppressed, and human lives squandered, of the many people who for centuries and still today are unable to surmount obstacles in life and flourish in fresh circumstances. It is one thing to sacrifice one's own life in voluntary self-offering; too many lives in the past and the present have been given up by force.

We climbed on, slowly and steadily, resting frequently for water. The sharp geological features became more pronounced, and the view behind us began to stretch into the far distance.

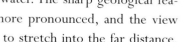

Left: The narrow tunnel.

Hebrew has a second word for desert, *midhbar*, from the root *dabhar*, which means "word" or "thing". Hebrew is a concrete, not an abstract, language, and always points to that which actually exists. In other words, the desert "speaks". This was becoming obvious as we toiled ever higher in a boiling sun. In such a place, we trusted and obeyed our guide absolutely. Speaking demands hearing, of course, but Hebrew has no separate word for "obeying". To hear is to obey: God speaks, and response neither requires nor allows a separate act of human will or choice. What the desert says is undeniable, and so it is between God and us.

Resting for nourishment, passing round sweet, fleshy dates, it was possible to recognise that the desert has other faces. Exodus 24 tells

Above: In the desert, as in life, you have to trust and obey your guide!

Below: On the rim of the Large Crater.

of the Israelite leaders and elders joining Moses on a high mountain, where they "saw God and ate and drank" (Exodus 24:10). Despite the physical difficulties, this uniquely awesome but beautiful place reflects the radiance of God's glory. We had watched the sun rise over this huge landscape, and the clouds dissipate, and now we sat together on sharp stones in very strong sunlight under a pure blue sky, as though under God's feet there was indeed a sapphire pavement (v.10).

THE SUMMIT

The last steep ascent required us to spread out and scramble up the last thirty feet or so, often on hands and knees. At the summit we found ourselves suddenly on a narrow ridge surrounding a huge and perfectly formed natural crater several miles across. We sat and pondered the awesome, breathtaking sight from the edge of Ha-Makhtesh Ha-Gadol, the "Large Crater", one of three similar features in the Negev. In geological terms, it is the circular rim of what was once a huge dome of sedimentary rock, now extensively collapsed and eroded. Other theories suggest an ancient volcano, or the fall of large meteors. But as the climax of that day's events, it was a magical moment, a genuine surprise and a truly spectacular sight. We sat, and ate and drank. The ravens circled over the heads of the climbers.

Our elation was mixed with trepidation, now contemplating a perilous descent down a slope that appeared impossibly steep. Our guide knew all the hidden paths, although a particularly difficult section required three climbers to ease the others down through a defile in the rocks. A rewarding moment, learning to trust not only our guide but also each other. In no time, we were back with our coach, which had come round the mountain to meet us, and lunch was quickly produced, and just as rapidly devoured.

Above: …we sat together on sharp stones in very strong sunlight under a pure blue sky …

Below: …on a superbly spirited Arab horse (see page 29).

Right: Cats at Kfar HaNokim catch scorpions we are told...

An hour's drive took us to the oasis of Kfar HaNokdim, just below the Dead Sea ridge, a Bedouin visitor centre. Under the camel-skin covers of a large communal tent we tried to rest during the hours of fiercest heat. Then, later in the afternoon, we travelled by camel a short distance into the fantastic desert landscape. Later, towards evening, we drove to a spectacular viewpoint overlooking the deep chasm of *wadi Tse'elim*, perhaps a model for the "valley of the shadow of death". It was a beautiful prospect from a safe

height, but a terrifying place for travellers, at the mercy of sudden flash floods and of marauding brigands. Haggai, the young Israeli manager of the centre, rode out to meet us on a superbly spirited Arab horse, and read, with equally boundless enthusiasm, the Hebrew text of Psalm 23, which, he assured us, was written in this very wadi! He then regaled us with Bedouin stories of more recent events, of dark secrets in the caves in these parts. Such stories are all middle, with no beginning or end, and run into each another without linear logic. By this time we had begun to forget our western habit of checking watches, learning that the one thing desert peoples have in abundance is time! The strong wind lessened just as the sun dipped below the horizon, and we remembered we had watched it rise together that morning, so long ago!

BEDOUIN HOSPITALITY

We returned in the dark for an evening of "Bedouin hospitality" around the fire, tea and coffee rituals, reclining at low tables, taking care to be culturally correct when eating with fingers. Conversation illuminated certain aspects of the Abraham tradition, and raised questions about particular exegetical questions. What was Sisera doing in Jael's tent (in Judges 4)? Breaking Bedouin taboo, it seems! We were allowed the luxury of a mattress and sleeping bag, and did manage some sleep in our communal tent, until two local cats chose to have a running battle up and down the roof sheets. By 5am the sky was reddening against the palm trees of the oasis and the backdrop of mountains.

Below: Conversation continues into the night in the tent of our Bedouin hosts.

6am - woke to this!

*Above: Dawn, and we wake
to this view.*

Chapter Four

INTO EGYPT

At 6.15am the sun rose suddenly, filling the red sky with white light, and the promise of heat. We prepared for a long drive south in the Negev today, through the barren rift valley of the Arabah towards the Red Sea. The jagged peaks of mountains rose on either side, but the desert is white and bare except for isolated groves of date palms and irrigated fruit trees. Eilat is a brash sun resort. Across the border in Jordan is Akabah, a busy port.

Although Eilat bristles with security devices of all sorts, the surrounding hills alive with masts, Taba over the Egyptian border offers a simpler and warmer welcome, with much stamping of forms and passports. This done, we clambered into a small fleet of land cruisers and moved off at a cracking pace along a good road hugging the shoreline, with the gorgeous blue waters of the Red Sea and miles of empty beaches just below. After a while the road begins to climb a steep and long ravine, before vehicles go off-road, swaying and bumping across the desert of southern Sinai. Two hours of this backbreaking progress took us to a narrow wadi, enclosed by steep sandstone cliffs on either side. In this dramatic setting, against a setting sun, we ate and drank round a fire, and a party of Bedouin on four camels turned up from nowhere, to share our meal and sell a few trinkets. We had seen no one since leaving Taba, but obviously we had not been alone!

Without mattress or tent (or cats!), travellers sleep on the sand, in brilliantly clear air, under a sky full of stars. Being an insulin dependent diabetic, I took care to keep my supply of extra carbohydrate close by. Unfortunately I was disturbed by the wildlife again. During the night I was woken by a rustling sound, and found by the light of a torch two small desert mice inside my bag enjoying the biscuits! Not much sleep again, then, but time for reflection. The mice belong here. Do I?

Three days into a desert journey. Travellers are quite safe in the company of others, but we are now at least two hours from the nearest tarmac road and moving still deeper into the wilderness tomorrow. Despite entering the desert in darkness, encountering its heat and its uncompromising nature, and enduring physical discomfort and strenuous effort, I did not feel out of place. We had seen sights of awesome beauty. The earth, the dust, the rocks, still warm from the day's heat, evoke a sense of re-acquaintance after some primeval parting, some basic affinity with the ground from which we are formed, especially this earth which bears few marks of human exploitation, only the crushing and shaping by ancient seismic forces and the long erosion by wind and water.

DESERT INSPIRATION

It is small wonder that the desert has always offered inspiration to religious people. This is where our ancient scriptures originated, and where the peoples of the book were formed. This is where religious people return for spiritual refreshment – a return to origins. It is also a place of fierce testing; physical, mental and spiritual. A place of stillness, of long silent waiting, of expectancy, just as the land thirsts for rain. A place too, of extremity and struggle, of aridity, desolation and abandonment. These opposites are written into the stories that originate here. So the desert stands at the very centre of the religious quest. A reminder that the world can be a very uncomfortable place in which to live. People can feel very alone at times, even when surrounded by others, and the world can seem very much against them.

From the fourth century onwards, Sinai developed as one of the important centres of Christian pilgrimage, alongside Bethlehem and Jerusalem. Some scholars now say that better historical sites for Israelite origins can be found in Saudi Arabia, but it matters little. Historical reconstruction is impossible, and the attempt to locate Sinai was not made until the fourth century after Christ. It is in the deserts of Palestine and Egypt that we can discover the roots of that Christian spirituality which emerged here at the close of the period of persecution. If martyrdom no longer happens in the West, and if Christian practice becomes lax and worldly, where can the cutting edge of faith be found? Our purpose in coming to the desert is not simply to view biblical locations, but to relive something of the authentic spiritual experience.

Below: We thought we were alone, but figures materialised as if out of nowhere.

Chapter Five

MOSES' MOUNTAIN

After an early cooked breakfast, we were soon on our way again. The jeeps scrambled over rocks and loose sand, sometimes almost foundering. Two hours later we rejoined the road, which continued through completely empty mountainous terrain for about 50 miles before we arrived at St. Catherine's monastery, ready for the ascent of Jebel Musa, the mountain of Moses. From below it looked all but impossible, rearing up several thousand feet. Some of the party chose camels, the rest walked around the huge sixth-century walls enclosing this most ancient of monastic settlements and found a winding path climbing the precipitous slope. Easier than it had first appeared, the effort was rewarded with ever-expanding views across a landscape of breathtaking grandeur. The hardest part is the final stretch leading to the summit, over 700 steps placed there by a very holy – and immensely strong!– monk. A fresh wind helped to relieve the heat and tiredness. On the summit, at 7,000 ft, is a small chapel, well stocked with icons, and a small mosque. I celebrated a simple Eucharist up here on this peak.

JEBEL CATERINA

The highest summit of the Sinai peninsula is now clearly seen, Jebel Caterina, at 8,000 ft, where the saint's body came to rest. In all directions appear forbidding, massive, rugged peaks of red granite, some of them capped with tiny buildings, the homes of hermits attached to the monastery. This inaccessible wilderness, a place of scorching summer sun and bitterly cold winter nights, came to be seen long ago as a sacred place. Early Christian monks soon found their way here. Persecution during succeeding centuries served to spread their fame, and southern Sinai became a place of pilgrimage for the leisured and pious. By the sixth century, the expansion and influence of this site prompted the Emperor Justinian to fortify the monastic enclosure with impenetrable granite

Above: Our exertions in reaching the top were nothing compared with the monk who built the steps.

Left: St Catherine's Monastery under the cliffs of Jebel Musa, the Mountain of Moses.

walls, some of which survive still. The monastery's vitality is splendid and surprising in such an arid, dead place. Symbolic, the monks say, of the flowering of the spiritual life that is possible through total repudiation of self-centredness, a literal form of self-offering.

The summit must be left in time to complete the two-hour descent to the monastery hostel before nightfall. The rocks change colour magnificently as the sun dips and the moon rises brilliantly in the clear sky. Tonight, in the monastery hostel, a rare treat - camp beds!

Above: For centuries pilgrims have endured the hazardous and arduous trek to this sacred spot.

Left: Inside St. Catherine's.

Chapter Six

ROCKS AND BONES

A large boulder just below the monastery wall served as a generous, round altar stone for an early Eucharist, led by a Lutheran pastor from the United States. It seemed an atavistic symbol for realities much older than our own religious traditions, and I remembered Luther's own antipathy towards sacrificial rites on medieval stone altars. But here, rock is the only available material.

Inside the walls, the monastery contains a magnificent collection of icons from many traditions and periods, including some of the earliest known. The "actual" Burning Bush, looking somewhat unhealthy, has its own chapel. A mosque huddles nearby; the local tribes of Bedouin have lived for centuries under the shelter of the monastery. There is also an extensive library that once contained one of the world's most precious manuscripts. The bell-tower, constructed in 1871, was a Russian recompense for the loss of this very early text of the Bible, "borrowed" in 1859 and never returned. This *Codex Sinaiticus* is now in the British Museum.

DEAD MONKS

The Charnel House is piled high with the skulls of dead monks, and, in a special place, the complete skeleton of Stephanos, resplendent in the robes of an abbot. The robes looked suspiciously less venerable than their former owner, so perhaps he is fitted out with new ones from time to time. I suspect that our hilarity at this scene indicated something of our ignorance of the tradition that venerates such things, but also our failure to grasp its spiritual depth. What seems merely quaint or fossilised to a western mind conceals its profound spirituality from those who spend their lives rushing everywhere. There is a timeless quality of life here which is somehow apparent in the rocks and the bones.

But we still had our timetable for the rest of the day! The jeeps, bumping and rolling along wadis and plains, are liable to break down and needed to be pushed out of the sand on several occasions. About midday we came across some strange structures in the middle of nowhere, a series of Bronze Age burial huts, with doors all facing west; another reminder of the timescale of the desert, and its ancient secrets. We finally lurched our way to a narrow and steep-sided wadi for a meal and songs around a campfire before, exhausted, sliding into sleeping bags.

Left: Bronze Age burial hut.

Right: Eyeless in the desert. The skulls of long-dead monks are piled high in the Charnel House.

Above: A desert mosque.

Chapter Seven

DESERT LEADERS — ABRAHAM AND MOSES

Up at 5.30am, and another beautiful day in prospect. Boiled egg and pitta bread for breakfast, then off at a fast pace down the wadi, and on to a seemingly endless plain, the mountains receding into the far distance on either side. After two hours or so, crossing this featureless expanse of glaring white, a small hut came into sight. We drew up, and a woman appeared, offering us small cups of hot, sweet tea. She was dressed from head to foot in sheer black, and only her eyes were visible, the rest of her face hidden behind a face veil. Her eyes smiled a welcome, but she seemed uneasy speaking to men.

Enjoying this rest from the uncomfortable riding of the jeeps, we noticed a small cloud of dust in the far distance, something travelling in our direction. In a few moments we could make out an old truck, moving fast. We watched as it rushed towards us, stopping sharply just in front of the small hut. Two men got out, and without a word moved to one side, taking off their shoes. Only then did I notice a small square of stones arranged on the ground, and an entrance marked on one side of the square through which the two passed before kneeling on the ground for prayers. It was midday. No doubt they had come from tending a flock somewhere. This expression of devotion in such emptiness was impressive. I dearly longed to join them.

After this, we reached the new road once again, taking us northward, skirting the shore of the Red Sea. We stopped for our own devotions on a beach near Nuweiba, where we held a Eucharist. An Anglican rite, in which the Roman Catholic priests present felt able to participate fully because they were allowed to recite the words of institution together with the presiding priest. To me a slightly odd device, but a welcome one if it enables some larger sharing among Christians. The mountains of Saudi Arabia loomed through the haze across the water.

THE DEAD SEA

Crossing back into the state of Israel, we were thankful for the smooth roads and an air-conditioned coach after the severe jolting hour after hour in the jeep. Our route led down to the Great Rift Valley, 1,200 feet below sea level. Visitors rarely bypass En Boqeq without a customary dip in the Dead Sea. The water here is quite unpleasant if it gets in the eyes or mouth, and showers are provided for washing it off afterwards, but the backdrop of the sheer, steep cliffs is magnificent. It is a long drive along the Dead Sea shore, but the setting sun and rising mist gave the Jordanian hills a wonderful colouring mirrored perfectly in the absolutely still water.

We have journeyed several hundred miles today. The granite mass of Sinai is truly spectacular, as is the Negev Highlands. The Negev we passed through today is dull by comparison, reminding me of an industrial spoil site, though it is all, of course, entirely natural. Somewhere in the heart of that desert Israel is building its own nuclear arsenal, and with it the potential to create new and more horrifying deserts. I am very tired. Neither the times spent in jeeps, nor the outward-bound aspects of the programme, seem to have taught me much about desert spirituality. But it is easy to become very romantic about the desert. The prayer of the desert is hard and slow, like the terrain itself.

Left: Only her eyes were visible...

What I have learned from these few days in the desert? We have spent much of the time travelling, and perhaps haven't spent enough time on foot. The desert has plenty of time, and only reveals itself to those who also have time. We had only a timetable.

As we arrive at the oasis of En Gedi, we are reminded of the tradition that the love poem known as the Song of Solomon originated here:

Who is this coming up from the desert
Leaning on her lover?...
Many waters cannot quench love;
Rivers cannot wash it away ...   (CHAPTER 8, VERSE 5)

A midrashic commentary later added this interpretation:

Who is this coming up from the desert? Israel's ascent is from the desert, her division into tribes is from the desert, the Torah is from the desert, the holy tent is from the desert, the Sanhedrin is from the desert, the priesthood is from the desert, the kingdom is from the desert... all good gifts that God bestows upon Israel come from the desert...

SIGNIFICANCE OF THE DESERT

Abraham and Moses provide models of faith and of leadership within desert contexts and culture. Jesus began his ministry in the desert too, crossing the Jordan (like the crossing of the Red Sea) at his baptism by John, and then heading off into the desert for his time of testing. The story of Jesus is written in some ways as an echo of the story of Moses. Neither ever forgot the desert.

Below: Among the bathers in the Dead Sea were some elderly Russian ladies who resolutely kept their clothes on for the occasion.

Abraham's story revolves around themes of possession and dispossession. He goes to "his own country" (Genesis 12:1), although a literal translation of his call is to go

Above: Young people are to be found everywhere waiting for lifts or buses. Every young person, male or female, must do National service. It is strange seeing young teenagers with guns. They are so young...

"to himself". In doing both, he makes the discovery of himself and of his God in the desert, the place (*midhbar*) where God speaks and whose word is incontrovertible, and the shimmering horizon (*shimmah*) to which he must be always moving. God invites him to move towards that which remains out of sight, because the call of God is always to an emptying of self and to a reaching out beyond self. The monks, the inheritors of Abraham in the Negev, continually respond to the same call while remaining in the desert.

Moses' story revolves around themes of oppression and release, and the determination to build a community that is capable of putting into actual practice, beyond the desert and beyond the monastery, this summons and promise of God. The history and tradition within which we live and by which we are being formed, as Christians, carry powerful echoes of this motif. So do the land and its peoples whom we encounter here today, in often distressing and violent ways.

The desert has a place in all our lives. We are always leaving and re-entering it. In so many ways it can be a very bare place, without compromise. But it takes time to see the desert. Look long enough, and you realise that those empty spaces of sand and rocks are actually full of life, and have so much to give.

Left: Distant view of Ein Gedi.

Chapter Eight

DESPOTS AND DISSIDENTS — HEROD AND THE ZEALOTS

As travellers move northwards, leaving the desert behind, it is possible to glimpse not only the physical places in which Jesus exercised his ministry, but also something of the social, political and religious contexts in which it was set. Recent years have seen an avalanche of books researching the life and times of Jesus. This is partly the reason for our visit, because Jesus can be adequately understood only against the background of the cultural milieu of that particular place and time. When I first began my own theological training in the 1960s, New Testament scholarship was still dominated by pessimism concerning the historical person of Jesus. It was then thought that the Gospels contain very little hard material relating to events in Jesus' life or his actual words. They tell us much more about how the earliest Christian communities came to understand, believe and preach about him. If you took this view, there would be little point in coming to the Holy Land to study the faith of the New Testament. Such a view, though not discredited, has since given way to a new optimism, based on fresh knowledge and understanding of Judaism in Palestine at the time of Jesus.

We are leaving the desert and entering what became the promised land. The rabbis said that the Torah was given to the Jewish people *outside* the promised land, during their time of dispossession. They could never claim that the Torah, and so their understanding of God, belongs exclusively to them alone. It belongs to all.

Between the desert and the promised land, we make a short detour. Between the desert figures of Abraham and Moses, and that of Jesus of Nazareth in Galilee, stands the imposing personality of Herod the Great, a kind of antitype of the others. His was a time of great crisis for leadership, the period of extensive Hellenistic influence in the countries of the Middle East. Herod the Great's stronghold at Masada, more than any of his other palaces, illustrates powerfully the despotic nature of his leadership. When the Israelite people eventually left their desert origins and patterns of leadership behind, and formed settled communities in Canaan, the desire for a king of their own was irresistible. It was a mistake that was to haunt them for many centuries. The prophets regularly criticised the leadership of the Israelite kings for their reversion to Canaanite behaviour. Herod was a Jewish king who ruled in Judea for his Roman masters from 37BC until 4AD, and for much

Above: The hills behind Masada.

of that time was separated from his people by fear and power, his isolation symbolised by the massive ramparts of Masada. It was built as a double defence, both against Cleopatra, his archrival as ruler of the Jews, and against revolts by his own people. He was caught between these two paradigms, Abraham/Moses and Caesar, but was drawn to both. He wanted absolute power and control; he also needed to make himself accessible in the manner of all Middle Eastern rulers, and of the Israelite kings who dispensed justice for the people in the gate, in the public place. The remains of his great throne room at Masada make this perfectly plain, both accessible and controllable.

I am struck by the fact that here, on the edge of the Judean desert, by the shore of the Dead Sea, we are standing at what was the easternmost boundary of the Roman Empire. Not long before, I had taken a similar party to view the remains of Hadrian's Wall, in

My first view of Masada - from a coach. A huge lozenge shaped rock
starting out of the edge of the Dead Sea

Northumberland, which marked the westernmost extent of Roman expansion and dom-
ination. An achievement, then and now!

Herod's career is a perfect instance of the delusions and corruptions of worldly power,
in contrast to the kingdom announced by Jesus, which is *in*, but not *of* (or better said, *from*)
this world. Maybe Jesus had Herod's career in mind in choosing to speak so often of God's
kingdom. His teaching undeniably continues the long story of the human struggle with the
temptations of wealth, power and control. When Jesus speaks of the nearness of God's
kingdom, he raises this question of leadership. Is it to be based on the Herodian model,
whose ultimate outcome is the all-powerful "divine Caesar"; or on the model of Abraham
and Moses, who were remembered as leaders close to the people and trusted by them? It
is clear that Herod's ambitious and unscrupulous regime was very much in the minds of
those who wrote the synoptic gospels. They tell a tale of two kingdoms, of two men called
"King of the Jews".

"MASADA SHALL NOT FALL AGAIN"

Since its first major archaeological exploration in the 1960s, Masada has attracted visitors
to the site of the last stand of the Jewish revolt until its final capture by the Roman army
under Flavius Silva after a long siege in 73AD. As such it became a powerful national symbol for modern Israelis, "Masada shall not fall again". It is easy to see how such an imposing outcrop with its seemingly impregnable fortress takes on this political and essentially
mythic character. Since then, however, Israeli politicians have led the political focus away
from the symbol of Masada, essentially a tale of Jewish people surrounded by enemies and
bent on suicide. Modern Israel is looking for new patterns of leadership, and forging reality from a different storyline. This illustrates the constant interplay between narrative and
history. Stories we tell about ourselves survive only to be superseded by something more

useful, and perhaps closer to historical reality. Historians, after all, are always in search of new facts. Similarly, our task as Christians is one of reformulation and renewal, constantly seeking fresh understanding. It is not in the nature of truth to stand still.

We drove round to the western side of Masada, from where the Roman army laid siege for more than a year. Their large walled encampments are still visible on the surface, and we walked up the massive siege ramp that eventually allowed them to take the site. According to Josephus Flavius, the last survivors had committed suicide at the instigation of their leader, Eleazar, rather than be taken by a foreign army.

Above: A Tristram's Grackle scrapes a living on scraps from tourists' picnics.

The flat top of Masada is almost half a mile in length, and bears much evidence of its successive occupations by Herod, by Zealots, and by Christian monks. The splendours of the royal palace and the king's private accommodation can still be traced in the few remnants of mosaic floors and painted rooms. Rough stone structures built by Zealots a hundred years after Herod reveal how a palace, built for the personal pleasure of one man, was turned into a stronghold for a community of a thousand people. It exemplifies the end of an era, a reminder of life between the times. Many suggest that our own time bears the same transitional character. Certainly Jesus himself lived between two great cultures.

The ruins of a very ancient synagogue still exist at Masada, predating all other Jewish remains elsewhere, and so of considerable historical importance, and the focus of intense debate. The benches are arranged on all four sides, designed to focus attention on the gathered community itself rather than on any other object or ritual focus. The foundations of a small side room, perhaps for housing Torah scrolls, suggest that this was a later addition. The Greek word *synagogue*, like its Christian equivalent *ekklesia*, means a gathering of people rather than a building.

We descended by cable car via the eastern slope, which offers magnificent views. The

The lady striding across the top of Masada looked very English. —

Right: The easy way up
Masada is by cable car.

Dead Sea contains much less water than it did, as is obvious from this height. It is possible to cross on foot at this point. Not a good idea, however, as the salty water can kill if swallowed. It contains no fish or other organism and it was once thought that no bird could even fly over it! Today, however, the attractive Tristram's Grackles (so called after a nineteenth century Anglican priest) are much in evidence; like black starlings with chestnut wing tips, they are doing very well out of each tour party waiting their turn for the cable car ascent.

BETWEEN THE TIMES

A brief respite from the midday heat in the air-conditioned coach as we moved on to Qumran, one of the most important archaeological discoveries of the twentieth century. Here, on a terrace overlooking the northern end of the Dead Sea, stand the remains of fortified community buildings, in all probability built on even more ancient foundations by the Jewish sect of Essenes sometime during the time of Herod the Great. Their response to life "between the times" had been to reject the Hellenising tendencies of the Jerusalem establishment and to live here, or in caves in the surrounding hills. Before their settlement was finally destroyed by the Romans in 68AD, they had hidden their precious scrolls containing the Hebrew scriptures and their own codes of discipline in the caves, not to be disturbed again until 1947 when the first discoveries were made.

   This sect set great store by religious purity, and I was fascinated by the remains of a large *miqveh,* or ritual bath, which I feel certain has much to tell us about the Judaic origins of Christian baptism. The practice of ritual immersion in "living" water is usually interpreted as running water, and many early Christian baptismal fonts were so arranged that river or spring water could flow through them. The original *miqveh*, however, was the sea itself, when God "miqvehed" or gathered the waters together into a whole system, teeming with life. Strict Jewish practice in the first century required complete immersion, performed not by a minister, passively, as in Christian ritual, but actively by the individual in the presence of a witness. Immersion had to be total, and therefore required the candidate to adopt a foetal position as the water covered the head. The imagery of rebirth is unmistakable. Intriguingly, it is claimed by some that the *miqveh* at Qumran was built over the site of a more ancient sacrificial altar. If so, it symbolises the transition from fire to water as the central religious motif of Judaism. Christianity inherits this theme, leaving behind the fire of Temple sacrifice, and finding the water of life in a thirsty land.

Controversies have raged recently about the nature of the community or communities that occupied this site before and after the time of Jesus. The archaeologists who first came to Qumran knew what they were looking for, and so identified the site as the home of a monastic community. One large room is still called a "scriptorium" although no trace of any scroll was ever found in it. Such premature conclusions fuelled suspicion, as did the air of secrecy that subsequently surrounded scholarly work on the Dead Sea Scrolls themselves. Whatever Qumran actually was, it illustrates perfectly the contemporary context of Jesus' coming to the desert, and his association with the ministry of John the Baptist. Although the New Testament authors do not explicitly mention Qumran, the formation of the Essene movement is undoubtedly in the background of the Gospel story. Here was a strict Torah observant and exclusive community choosing internal isolation as a way of being the true Israel, and awaiting the coming of a Messiah. Contrary to the claims of some scholars, no New Testament texts were found here. Yet several idioms are common to both, and occur nowhere else, such as the well-known phrases "the poor in spirit" and "hungering and thirsting for righteousness".

Above: The hills of Jordan across the Dead Sea.

The sun was at its height as we stood inside a partially restored building on the site, drinking copious amounts of water, and seeking the thin sliver of shade afforded by the walls. As we stood together in what might have been a kind of refectory, someone read extracts from the community's manual, detailing the regulations surrounding its common meals. Such meals were sacred, not because of any holiness in the food itself, but because of the religious vow which bonded the community together. Those who broke such a vow were excluded from the community meal. Although Christianity's eucharistic theology developed differently, this same tradition could well be present in the gospel accounts of Jesus' last supper with his community of disciples. Several forms of Judaism were developing in the first century, defining themselves in different ways as the authentic people of God, and people of the time were perfectly aware of the religious options available. Qumran offered a perfectionist flight to the desert. The Pharisees offered another exclusive way of being Israel according to strict religious codes of practice. The Sadducees sought to preserve Jerusalem's cultic system from outside interference. The Zealots offered a nationalistic militarism. And out of Galilee a new way arose.

Above: Unconsciously, we gravitated towards the shade.

Beyond the ancient oasis of Jericho, the road leads northwards through the Jordan valley, and soon enters the territory of the West Bank, once part of Jordan, occupied though never annexed by Israel since 1967, and now partly under the administration of the Palestinian Authority. The road skirts the main urban settlements of Ramallah and Nablus, and stays close to the course of the river, a small stream in a very wide plain. One rusty trig point survives from the days when the new boundaries were defined by the United Nations in 1948. Today, Israeli army checkpoints guard the border. Either side of the road along its entire length, regular patrols survey a corridor of swept sand. In truth, there is very little human or economic activity in this hard and mostly uncultivated land, nor much traffic on the road, just a few groups of storks flying northward. Occasionally the remnants of earlier UN refugee camps can be seen; the refugees of 1948 were further displaced after 1967. Near Jericho the Palestinian police seem to have established a training camp of sorts, but the whole area seems unnaturally quiet. Another desert.

Below: Double staircase Miqveh.

We travelled fast, and the aridity and desolation of the West Bank soon gave way to the irrigated greenness of the valley of Jezreel. We made a brief stop at Beth She'an (or Scythopolis) where the remains of a Byzantine town, including an enormous ampitheatre, have been excavated. The design of sports stadia has not changed much in 2000 years! The dark basalt foundations of these huge buildings gave the first hint of our approach to Galilee.

Approaching a crossroads, two police cars had just arrived at the scene of an accident. Two vehicles had collided. No one seemed seriously hurt, which seemed surprising, given the generally appalling standard of driving. The fact that they were military police cars also seemed unsurprising, given the very large number of young men and women under arms in Israel. What caught my eye was the Hebrew phrase on the cars, *mishtorah shebarith*, from *sabaoth*, usually translated in our liturgies as "hosts", but actually meaning "armies". We just happened to be passing Mt. Gilboa, where Saul and Jonathan perished after the defeat of their armies. The echoes of this part of the long story are never far away.

We journeyed further northwards to cross the Jordan at the point where the Sea of Galilee flows into the Jordan. The local kibbutz has provided a stopping place here for Christian pilgrims, who arrive here in great numbers for baptismal services. The water teems with fish, possibly attracted by nearby sewage outfalls. It is a sadly uninviting site for a baptism. Our very first introduction to the holy land of tourism, and its souvenir mentality! The Jordan river is not just water - it is a transition. This much is true of the Baptism of Jesus, even if this seems an unlikely spot at which to reflect on it. We have moved from brown to green, from Palestine to Israel, from desert to country, from Judea to Galilee.

Below: Mass baptism for pilgrims.

Chapter Nine

Above: The basilica at Nazareth.

THE REAL JESUS — NAZARETH AND SEPPHORIS

Nazareth is today an extensive modern city stretching over a wide hillside, with a predominantly Israeli Arab population and an expanding Jewish sector. Its Christian population was also once very numerous, but is now declining, as it is all over modern Israel. St. Margaret's Hostel, an Anglican foundation, once an orphanage, offers cool rooms with showers to wash off the dust of the desert, and a bar with cold local beers. We slept well, and were woken by the call to prayer from several local mosques, all broadcast by loudspeaker, followed by the Angelus from the bell of the Roman Catholic basilica. The hostel occupies a commanding position overlooking the old town, the view from the balcony dominated since 1968 by the said church. Although its massive size seems out of all proportion to the tiny Roman Catholic population of the Holy Land, its presence here signifies the importance of this place for all Christians. Here Jesus was conceived, here he was brought up, here his ministry began. An ancient Jewish saying suggests that God whispers all the world's secrets to the foetus, but they are all lost at birth and we spend the rest of our lives rediscovering them.

Walking down the steep hill into the town, we passed shops and stalls beginning to open for the day. The traders seemed very enterprising, as they surely must be to survive, trying their sales pitch in French, German and Italian. Two small boys outside a tiny sweet shop, however, guessed that we might be American. They seemed surprised when we said we were English. "Well, you speak American!" they said.

BASILICA OF THE ANNUNCIATION

Not far away, the Basilica of the Annunciation rears up suddenly at a street corner like a beached lighthouse, distinctively faced with limestone and red marble banding. The building strongly reflects the theology of the Second Vatican Council - it encloses the whole people of God, but it remains powerfully pyramidal in form. It is a hierarchical statement. Yet because it is a concrete shell containing a host of individual set pieces, anyone could find something in it worth taking away. Constructed in the 1960s after Pope Paul VI's visit to the Holy Land, every Roman Catholic community was invited to submit panels interpreting the Annunciation theme, and the results now surround both the church and cloister. The interior of the high lantern is supposed to evoke an unfolding flower, a motif that does not lend itself easily to concrete. (Jerome, apparently, and half-correctly, thought the Hebrew root *nzr* meant "blossom"; in fact, its meaning is closer to "branch" or "shoot"). The building is uncompromisingly modern in design and materials, a giant concrete hangar on two levels, enclosing, at its heart, the remnants of a tiny cave. In fact, the basilica encloses one building within another, and at its heart is a house. It is

not the first church here, and the remains of earlier structures are also to be found inside. The cave itself, the object of centuries of devotion, has been venerated almost out of existence. The reason is made clear by the tiniest addition to the biblical text on the altar in the little grotto: 'Verbum Caro hic factum est' - the Word was made flesh *here*. Christians have long used this place as a powerful focus for contemplating the mystery of incarnation. Regardless of the precise identification of the historical location, the historical dimension is of absolute importance. After all, if it did not happen in history, how can it happen in the present, and in every Christian community, and with me? as Meister Eckhardt said. Historical facts, however, cannot in themselves provide any adequate basis for faith. Faith, by definition, does not seek guarantees. There seems little reason to doubt, however, that in a cave house somewhere in the tiny hamlet that existed here in the first century, Jesus was brought up. Here he found his identity and vocation, and began to discover life's secrets.

Below: Shops and stalls are just opening as we walk down the steep hill into town.

Underneath the main church is a small museum of finds from the excavations during the mid 20th-century building work. We saw marks made by early pilgrims, several exquisite Crusader-period stone capitals never actually used and therefore not weathered, and another cave house (perhaps the neighbours?) dating from the first century or earlier. Its plan conforms to the typical early Palestinian type, with two rooms, outer and inner. Animals would have been kept in the rear of the cave for warmth during the cold winter months. This seems to fit the description of Jesus' birth (though set in Bethlehem, of course) given in Luke 2:7, where the Greek word often translated as "inn" (*kataluma*) might refer to the outer room of such a house. The manger could then have been inside the cave, assuming, of course, that Jesus was born during the winter, which does *not* fit Luke's story. Sheep were kept in the fields after harvest, when there would have been something for them to eat. There is not much grass around Bethlehem!

The house of the White Sisters, a French order, is nearby, and they welcomed us warmly, and showed us their own excavations, which reveal another cave house cut into the rock, with evidence of later Christian veneration. Underneath this is a marvellous example of a Jewish tomb, with a preparation room, and a stone for sealing a small rear chamber. Could this be, the sisters wondered, the lost Church of the Nutrition - and so the house of the holy family?

The Greek Orthodox Church of St. Gabriel, just down the road, is entirely different. It is built over a spring, presumably where Mary drew water; in other words, at its heart is the open air! Not anymore, although the scale is homely and the welcome friendly. Inside, the lavish provision of modern icons fits well within the overall scheme, and they provide an intimate setting that invites reflection - and the lighting of candles.

Nazareth is a noisy, bustling town, full of traffic, prosperous, westernised and predominantly Arab. The new Jewish settlements are on the surrounding hills. A felafel lunch is a splendid feast - all kinds of salads, dressings and vegetables with pitta bread and

Above: A shower and a beer are immediately refreshing.

Waiting for the Bank to open, Nazareth

kebabs, followed by sliced oranges. How do we interpret what is, according to very strong Christian tradition, the hometown of Jesus? There are various odd clues in the New Testament.

When told by Philip that the man foretold by Moses and the prophets had been found, and that it was Jesus the son of Joseph from Nazareth, Nathaniel exclaimed, "Can anything good come from Nazareth?"(John 1:46). The place may have had a reputation for lax observance of Torah. Why does Matthew's gospel quote an unknown prophetic source, "He shall be called a Nazarene"(Matthew 2:23)? Nazareth is certainly not mentioned in the Hebrew scriptures, so why does Luke's gospel have a Nazareth family coming south to Bethlehem? And why does Matthew's gospel have a Judean family going north to Galilee as refugees? Some speculations are possible. If the root form, *nzr*, is taken literally to mean "branch", it might imply that the place was known as the home of a particular "branch" or sect of messianic Judaism, well known at the time but subsequently forgotten. Perhaps this "branch" of the "tree" of Jesse, in Judea, was held to be unorthodox because it came to believe that the Messiah would come from their family. One might conjecture that the whole clan at some stage was forced to move northwards, and settled near the large town of Sepphoris. It is not beyond the bounds of historical possibility that Jesus grew up in a strict and non-conformist milieu. Returning later to Nazareth as a budding teacher and speaking publicly in the local synagogue one Sabbath (the episode recorded in Luke 4), his own clan would have understood his choice of reading from the Isaiah scroll. They knew what was written there about God planting his own chosen shoot (Isaiah 60:21), a branch prophecy they would have applied to themselves. The local hero had

returned. But Jesus disappointed them, and things got very nasty. No doubt they blamed it all on Sepphoris, where Jesus would have encountered broader interpretations and Hellenistic values. Jesus was a true southern Galilean who had learned to associate with people beyond this narrow religious circle, and was able to relate to the wider context of Greek culture. Maybe he even spoke Greek himself. We are not told by the gospel writers that Jesus ever went to Sepphoris - or to Tiberias, for that matter - the two most important towns at the time. It is inconceivable that he did not.

Right: A Crusader fort now tops the dig at Sepphoris.

ZIPPORI

All this exciting surmising made me look forward eagerly to our next stop - the excavations at Zippori, an Israeli national park, known to the Greeks as Sepphoris, and the Romans as Diocaesarea (the city of Jupiter and Caesar). It was here that the Mishnah, the oral Torah, was eventually collated and written down, about 200AD. The site, which began to be excavated from the 1980s, lies only four miles from Nazareth on a 1,000-foot hill overlooking the broad Bet Netofa valley to the north, which has always carried the main routes inland from the coast. It is a strategic site; perhaps the model for Jesus' image of the city set on a hill that cannot be hidden. In any case, the Hebrew root *zpr* carries the meaning of "a bird settling" (on a hill), according to the Babylonian Talmud. From the site of the city's theatre, surveying the wide horizon below, it is obvious what a significant city this must have been, called by Josephus Flavius the "ornament of all Galilee". In his day, sometime after 70AD, it must have been a fine metropolis of colonnaded streets, elegant villas, aqueducts, a forum and a spectacular theatre, and home to some 30,000 inhabitants. The Romans had made it the capital of Galilee in 55BC, but the army destroyed it in 4BC after putting down a Jewish revolt here. Throughout the lifetime of Jesus, Herod the Great's son Antipas was rebuilding it on a large scale to serve as a major power base in his tetrarchy of Galilee and Peraea, one of a string of Greco-Roman cities in the region. Surely Jesus must have come here? But any visits are not recorded, perhaps because the gospel texts, at least as we have them, reflect the conflicts between church and synagogue in the first century when they were being compiled. Both Sepphoris and Tiberias were well known as Jewish centres, especially after the destruction of Jerusalem in 70AD. We must remember that the gospels provide only fragmentary accounts of the actual life of Jesus, and the episodes that are recorded are included to serve the gospels' chief purpose, which is theological and evangelical. Did Jesus learn his trade here? The vast scale of the construction project after 4AD must have provided hundreds of jobs for local skilled workers and technicians. Luke's gospel has it that Joseph was a tekton, some kind of "technician", perhaps not literally a carpenter, but a worker or craftsman in stone or wood. If so, he and his son would have found plenty of work in Sepphoris.

We were able to muse on these questions over a coffee, served, to our surprise and pleasure, by a woman who had moved here from Sunderland! Some of us who know the new city of Sunderland reminisced with her about the old days on Wearside; talk about the old music hall at the Empire Theatre there drew my attention back to the ruins of a very different auditorium set in the side of the hill on which we were sitting.

THE THEATRE

The theatre at Sepphoris was huge, a splendid example of its type, with seating capacity for 4,500 people. Some authorities date it to the period of Antipas, others to the end of the first century. It is now under reconstruction, with white limestone seating as it might once have been now covering part of the exposed rock foundations. The theatre represented the centre of Greek culture and religion, and all the major cities of the region would have had one, usually well sponsored by the rich and the powerful. It is common in Jewish literature to read of attempts by the orthodox to prevent attendance at such theatres – a sure sign that Jews of the period did attend! Perhaps it is not too fanciful to suggest that the dramatic force of so many of Jesus' parables might have been drawn from his knowledge of the classical stage. The term "hypocrite", often used by Jesus, literally means "one who plays a part", an actor, and so by derivation comes to mean one who pretends or deceives, who merely plays a part in religious observance. Is this an indication that Jesus himself attended theatres or was acquainted with the performing arts? It is difficult to avoid the conclusion that this large and cosmopolitan city, so close to Nazareth, must have formed a significant part of Jesus' early life. It points to the conclusion that Jesus was well versed and took part in the religious debates and political

Below: The theatre at Sepphoris, not far from Nazareth, is under reconstruction.

controversies of his day. The real point of so many of his stories is illuminated more sharply when set against the background Jesus must have known so well - the "real politik" of Roman occupation, the military campaigns, the corruption of government, the wealth and display of the landowners, the hardship and poverty of the peasants, the tax collectors, the price of a good piece of wood, the actors in the theatre, and, most important of all, relations between the Jewish people and the "pagans".

Just below the café where we were sitting was a small fig tree. I was reminded of Nathaniel, whom Jesus first noticed standing under one such tree (John 1:48). Later, he recognised Jesus as a Rabbi or Teacher. We are often told to think of Jesus as a rough carpenter, a rustic countryman from the backwoods of Galilee, calling uneducated fishermen to be his disciples, but these common assumptions need to be challenged. Many references in the gospels indicate that Jesus was well known as a teacher of exceptional erudition who was sought out for his original and unconventional interpretation of Jewish tradition and practice. The fact that Jesus did not appear in public before the age of 30 suggests that he conformed to the conventions of that period, though we are told of his intellectual ability at an early age (Luke 2: 46). Like other outstanding teachers of the day, Jesus gathered a circle of disciples, instilling in them strict discipline and itinerancy, teaching orally in synagogues and elsewhere, and committing nothing to writing. The idea that Jesus was uneducated stems from an episode recorded in John 7, when the Jerusalem elite tries to brand him as a country hack. Jesus was a Galilean, at a time when an emerging northern school challenged the supremacy of the great Jerusalem teachers. They were jealous, no doubt, of his fame and ability, and threatened by his strictures on their cherished traditions. Jesus has always issued challenges to the powerful and support for the disadvantaged!

We spent as much time as possible exploring this fascinating site. There is so much to see, and to interpret, layered over from successive periods of history. It was becoming clear that Jesus had lived and travelled in a sophisticated urban culture, and his teaching needs fresh examination when set against what we can discover about his own context, cultural environment and social background. His visits here may not be recorded, but Sepphoris may hold important new keys to understanding the world in which Jesus grew up, lived, worked and taught.

MARY'S HOME?

Just below the ancient town is a house said to be that of Anna and Joachim, the parents of the mother of Jesus. Later (fifth century) Christian communities came to believe that Mary was brought up here! Nearby are the tombs of rabbis from the third century. Streets and buildings from the later Roman, Byzantine and Crusader periods are all in evidence. It seems amazing to us that, for example, Christian sites and rabbinic tombs could have been preserved by later Muslim occupants, but so it was. The hostility among the three great religions we know so well is a modern phenomenon, the product of crusades, imperialism and nationalism. For centuries, Jews, Christians and Muslims lived peaceably together.

Most stunning of all the remains at Zippori is the preserved mosaic floor of a *triclinium*, the dining room of a Roman period villa, dating possibly from the early third century. A series of scenes depicting the cult of Dionysius surrounds an almost perfectly preserved mosaic portrait of a woman, perhaps the owner of the villa. Whoever she is, the publicists have dubbed her the "Mona Lisa of Galilee". The sheer quality of this image helps us to imagine something of the luxury and magnificence of the meals consumed here, as guests reclined on three sides of the room (hence its name). The positions for the couches round the room can be easily seen, and reminds me that the last supper of Jesus was also taken in this reclining posture. In Roman culture, only free people were entitled to eat in this way – slaves ate standing. This is one more small but surprising reminder that when we go seeking insight into the origins of Christianity, we often find them in the synthesis of Jewish fundamentalism and Greco-Roman art and philosophy!

It had been a long tiring day. As we left the site and made towards our coach, a young Israeli soldier, a machine gun slung over his shoulder (soldier and gun are never parted) stopped me and asked whether we could give him a lift. I was severely rebuked by the Arab driver for making a positive response to this request. Apparently it is illegal (and punishable by imprisonment) for Arabs to pick up Israeli soldiers, and equally so for the latter to accept lifts from Arabs. A jarring experience in such a place.

The coach travelled into the barren hills and more difficult terrain of northern Galilee. In the fading light the lines of the hills against the sky looked very beautiful. The existence of some Christian-Muslim villages in this area, very active in building communities and reclaiming land, is a small sign of hope for the future. After dark we arrived in Safed, to find our hotel almost on the summit of the hill with commanding views. From the fifteenth century this was a Spanish Jewish settlement. We are only ten miles from the Lebanon border, and tomorrow we plan to move across the border with Syria, and into the occupied territory of the Golan.

Left: The haunting image of a woman captured on a mosaic floor in a Roman villa at Sepphoris.

Right: Israeli tank memorial.

Chapter Ten —

BORDERS AND BOUNDARIES

nother hot, bright day began with yoghurt, eggs, cheese and salad. By daylight we now realised our position, having climbed last night to a considerable height. We drove to a lookout spot to begin orientation for the day, looking down the rift valley to the Sea of Galilee glinting in the sun some 3,500 ft. below, and then up at the snow-capped peak of Mt. Hermon away to the north. There is also a large army base and airstrip, and many armed soldiers.

We stopped at a kibbutz near Hazor to view pieces from the excavations there. The Canaanite objects are all very small, figurines, tablets, and some charming carved lions. I wondered why the prophets and others protested so vigorously about "carved images". These objects were not "gods" but probably representations of priests or shrine guardians. Someone suggested that their modern equivalent could be "This is a sacred place, please respect it", like the notices posted for tourists at every religious site today. Ancient temples were built as houses for God, but much biblical literature was anxious to dispel the idea that the transcendent God actually lived in the Jerusalem Temple. The God whom no place on earth could possibly contain chose to place his "Name" there to establish his presence, but was not confined to any single place (Deuteronomy 12:5,11, Ezra 6:12).

We moved on to Tel Dan, within 100 yards of the original borders with Lebanon and Syria. The mound of the Tel formed the Israeli front line before 1967, and the remains of trenches still cut through this ancient site. Today there is a nature reserve which we explored, and where I caught glimpses of a most beautiful Smyrna kingfisher, with its red beak and iridescent blue feathers. The spring of the River Jordan bubbles up here, and we drank the water as it rushed and foamed over the rocks, sparkling in the sun. Just beyond the spring is a line of barbed wire, and beyond that a minefield. The bird song was periodically interrupted by firing from the military ranges nearby.

We clambered onto the Tel itself, the ruins of an Israelite city of the biblical period, perhaps dating from the reigns of Jeroboam or Ahab, its gate system built over the older Canaanite city of Laish. The gate complex is similar to that at Beersheba, and the repeated biblical expression "from Dan to Beersheba", obviously meaning the extremities of biblical Israel, seems fitting. But what is more surprising for those who take biblical history at its face value is the existence in Dan of a holy place of massive size, built with ashlar blocks, and with steps leading up to an enormous platform, the site of an altar. Many of the details conform closely to the dimensions and regulations laid down in the Bible for the Jerusalem Temple. But those texts suggest that there is only one Temple, and that it is in Jerusalem! So why is there another one here, and why is it not mentioned? The city of Dan was for centuries identified as the place of idolatrous worship, after the northern tribes rebelled against Rehoboam, son of Solomon, and crowned Jeroboam their king. He, fearful lest his subjects should defect after making pilgrimage to Jerusalem, set up this rival sanctuary.

TENSION

Back on the road, we passed kibbutzim surrounded by more barbed wire and watchtowers. The roadsides are littered with rusted military vehicles of all kinds, kept as memorials to the Jewish dead. Modern pieces of public sculpture also proliferate, all gaunt angular projections of metal or stone – reminders that this is still the Israeli front line. It is difficult to know where the real borders are. Maps showing the internationally agreed boundaries of the state of Israel are not published here. All Israeli maps show the occupied territories as though they were legally within the state of Israel. At some point we passed into occupied Syria and drove up into the Golan Heights. We came this far to visit a site tentatively identified as Gamla, the place of yet another violent confrontation between the Roman army and Jewish defenders in 67AD. It is a place to capture the imagination. The town was built on a formidable ridge with a remarkable crest and steep ravines carrying rushing waters down either side, and with homes constructed one above another. We entered the ruins through a breach made by the Romans (at least, a large notice claims it to be so) in the largely still-standing wall. The ground is littered with what could easily be Roman stone shot. Vultures circled overhead, eerily evocative of the gruesome story recounted by Flavius Josephus.

The major archaeological find here is the earliest known synagogue in the Holy Land. It is such a perfect example that until recently some doubted its identification, preferring to understand it as a Greek council chamber. It has benches on three sides, a Torah cupboard and reading platform on and dirt floor that would once have been carpeted. Externally there is clear evidence of a *miqveh* (which cannot have been of simple design on such a steep slope) with plastered sides. It is very difficult to make conclusive statements about Jewish religious practices and social customs in the time of Jesus, because most written sources post-date the first century. But here the dating is clear, and provides early

Jewish evidence for ritual purification that obeys all the later regulations in the Mishnah and Talmud. We read a few psalms and a midday Kaddish - then a *very* stiff climb back to the bus.

Driving round the hill and back down to the lake, we halted next at Kursi. Byzantine tourist guides identified the site as the Gadara mentioned in Mark 5, and even the cliff from which the herd of Gadarene pigs jumped to their deaths can be pointed out! The more likely origin of the site is the grave of the demoniac, commemorated by a fifth-century church and monastery of enormous interest. Although much restored, the classical plan is evident, with atrium, diaconium, apse, baptistery and colonnaded nave, most of which is covered with mosaics of enormous variety.

The lakeside road hugs the shore on a narrow strip of land beneath the Golan, fringed with palms and crowded beaches. The hills are of limestone, covered with light-coloured grass, a contrast to the hills on the north and west of the lake, where the limestone has a

Below: Galilee from Gadara.

covering of much darker basalt. Looking across the lake, so still and blue today, I recalled the episodes in the gospels in which Jesus crosses the lake by boat. That was a cultural journey, a crossing of more than physical distance. In Jesus' day, on the west side was the district of Galilee with its strongly Jewish population, and his own home territory. On the east side were the Gentile communities of the Decapolis, without much Jewish presence. This stark contrast makes it surprising that Jesus is said to have crossed the lake so often, and to have repeated his activities in both communities. Despite the gospel writers' concern to emphasise Jesus' mission to Israel, this is an indication of Jesus' desire also to move into foreign territory and to explore his outreach into a culture other than his own. His overriding purpose in doing so, it seems, was to proclaim the good news of the kingdom of heaven, but so much is lost in the translation of those few words. "Heaven" is a euphemism for God, and "kingdom" represents the reign of God that knows no frontiers of nation or culture. But the phrase "the one who proclaims the good news" is conveyed by a single word in both Greek and Hebrew. An English translation implies "something done" (ie proclaimed) with "some other thing" called "good news", as though the good news is a kind of commodity that can be acquired, learned and passed on. Not so. It is all one thing. The doing always lies in the being, and the good news is either implicit in the person living it, or it does not exist at all.

Swinging round the northern end of the lake means taking in the ever-changing views of the lake and the beaches from which Jesus taught, and skirting the towns of the so-called "evangelical triangle". Just east of Capernaum, where Jesus had made his home after leaving Nazareth, the road crosses the Jordan river on a girder bridge. In Jesus' time this point marked the border crossing between the Galilee ruled by Antipas and the northern region of Trachonitis and Iturea ruled by his brother Philip. Maybe it was here the tax collectors sat, collecting tolls for the Galilean government, and evidently taking a cut for themselves as well. The reason Jesus had so much to do with tax collectors, as well as other social outcasts, was because he was always crossing borders and boundaries of every description.

Tonight I read straight through St. Mark's gospel with a map in front of me, and pieces of the jigsaw began to come together. What we know as the biblical period is in fact a small slice of history, and the Old Testament is a *southern* production from Jerusalem, and much reading between the lines is necessary. I gained a stronger impression than ever before of a Galilean ministry followed by a final trip south to Jerusalem. Jesus has to be understood always against the background of the longer story, with all its inherent bias.

Our driver spoke of more deaths in the West Bank today as the Israeli army again clashed with Palestinian demonstrators. The borders and boundaries here are still so difficult to cross.

Left: The snows of Hermon to the north.

Right: A mosaic in the church at Tabgha shows two ducks perched in a lotus leaf.

Chapter Eleven

JESUS' MOUNTAIN

O ne of the most popular of all tourist sights associated with the Galilean ministry of Jesus is the so-called Mount of the Beatitudes. The phrase "Sermon on the Mount", a nineteenth century appellation for the famous collection of the sayings of Jesus in Matthew 5-7, served to focus attention on Jesus' teaching at this topographic point. With the sun shimmering on the still waters of the lake, all the places associated with the ministry of Jesus came within view. The church here dating from 1938 was designed by Barluzzi and paid for, apparently, by Mussolini. It is quite simple and handsome, containing much polished marble and hints of art deco, with an octagonal gallery designed for meditation on the eight beatitudes. Walking in this circle is itself a reminder not to get stuck at one place; the integrity of life in the kingdom of God lies in the whole, not the parts.

Right: We walk down to the Sea of Galilee, to meditate on Jesus' teachings.

Above: Galilee, the focus of Jesus' ministry.

So familiar from childhood stories and hymns, the Sea of Galilee is a part of everyone's very first encounters with Jesus. The whole ministry of Jesus was focused around these shores. It is, of course, not a sea at all, but a small lake, merely fifteen miles in length. It bears many names, including Genneseret, Gennesar, Tiberias, and today, as in the Old Testament, the Lake of Kinnereth. One name it never had is "Syrian Sea", popularised by the American Quaker poet John Greenleaf Whittier in the hymn *Dear Lord and Father of mankind*. Those famous verses about quietist piety are drawn from a lengthy and peculiar poem about drug taking and the avoidance of sensuality in worship, although they seem to have a powerful effect on the way English-speaking Christians understand Jesus, and his ministry here. It does need some revision!

NEW BEGINNING

We walked down the hill towards the road at the edge of the lake, moving slowly and silently. In early spring there is a profusion of wild flowers in the long green grass, which brings to mind Jesus' sayings about the flowers of the field in Matthew 6. In summer the grass is bleached dry and yellow in the hot sun, and was more reminiscent of the harder sayings about false prophets and bad trees in Matthew 7. Matthew places this section of teaching on a mountain, a high point literally and figuratively, because he wants to establish a relationship and a contrast with the figure of Moses. Jesus, the new Moses, offers a new way of establishing God's rule in people's lives, not by issuing proscriptive or prescriptive legislation, but through a new beginning. In the Beatitudes, all the centrally important things are reversed. The dispossessed peoples of the earth are blessed. The sorrowful will be consoled. The gentle shall prevail. The persecuted shall be vindicated. If Sinai was a mountain of exclusion, this is a mountain of inclusion. This is for everyone. And the challenge that it poses is as vivid and strong today as it ever was.

Sitting in the shade of olive trees halfway down the hill, despite the parable at the end of the "sermon" about the rain and wind demolishing the house built on poor foundations, it is difficult to imagine that it ever rains here! Over to the west in the distance, the unmis-

Capernaum Synagogue: Crowds of yellow-hatted tourists looking like chicks, flocking to their guide.

Right: Capernaum grind-stone — a local style which became popular throughout the whole country. Made from basalt.

takable outline of the Horns of Hattin can be seen, the place of the final defeat of the Crusaders by Saladin in 1187. This was another kingdom without firm foundations, and also another place without water. It is said that the Crusader armies were demoralised by lack of water and easily defeated

At the foot of the slope lies Tabgha, an ancient site of pilgrimage. The sea has receded from the ancient fishing towns of Jesus' day, but the tide of pilgrims here is endless. Two churches cater for them. The Benedictine church of the multiplication of the loaves and fishes (what a splendid excuse for a compound German noun, *Brotvermehrungskirche*) contains marvellous ancient and reconstructed mosaics, somewhat oddly depicting birds and flora of the Nile delta. Two ducks in a lotus flower — the perfect honeymoon! Below the altar stands the stone venerated as the place where Jesus placed the bread and fish, as recounted in Mark 6.

Farther along the road, a Franciscan church overshadows some ancient steps, long associated with the Spanish nun, Egeria, who first made Holy Land pilgrimages popular in the fourth century. A basalt chapel of little architectural merit now encloses the outcropping stone identified as *Mensa Domini* (the Lord's Table) on which the risen Jesus cooked breakfast (John 21). Chunky stained glass dapples it with colour. On busy days, masses and services are held in the grounds on a tightly organised timetable. As waves gently lap the shore, birds wheel above, and chanting and singing rise in a host of languages on the still air. The calm is frequently and noisily interrupted by yet more pilgrims disgorged from yet more coaches, all anxious to collect their very own bottle of Galilee water before the tour moves on to the next site.

A short distance away is Nof Ginosaur, a lakeside kibbutz that sports a Galilee Museum. A few years ago, when the water level in the lake was low, an ancient fishing boat was discovered in the mud, and now lies preserved in a tank. It is an interesting and impressive survival, about 25 feet in length and 8 feet wide and dated to somewhere between 100BC and 100AD. Goldfish swim in the tank to eat the algae that would otherwise destroy the wood.

GALILEE AT THE TIME OF JESUS

Jesus seems to have made Capernaum, then a thriving trading town and fish market, a semi-permanent base during his travels around the towns and villages in this part of Galilee. A few miles away in the hills lie the ruins of Chorazin, and Bethsaida was on a plain close by, now silted up. But Capernaum offers by far the most interesting and intriguing glimpses into the daily life of Galilee at the time of Jesus, and of subsequent generations of Christians. There are no *miqva'oth* here, however; ritual bathing would have been carried out in the lake, then much closer to the town than it is now. And from these beaches, (and perhaps also a harbour), some of those Jesus chose to be his disciples plied their trade. The fact that they were able to leave their boats with the hired men (Mark 1:21) implies that they and their families were boat owners, and not the uneducated simpletons they are sometimes imagined to have been. Was Jesus himself poor? Or did he choose to join the poor?

Above: The most famous synagogue thronged with tourists.

In the excavated remains of the town, the basalt foundations of small homes are clearly visible, built around courtyards where many basalt grindstones have been found. One such home, considerably larger than the others and displaying to the untutored eye an incredibly complex floor plan, is now covered over by what is surely a contender for the ugliest church building in Christendom. The Franciscans who own this site, and who have been largely responsible for its archaeological exploration, very plausibly identify this area with Peter's house. Originally just as tiny and insignificant as all the others, it must have been developed by successive generations of Christians from a very early house church into a large octagonal basilica by the fifth century. It seems reasonable to suppose that they did so because the earliest Christian community here knew it had been Peter's house. Numerous finds and graffiti also point to this conclusion. When Egeria came here, she saw such a house, and was told by her guides exactly what Franciscans repeat today. Unlike us, she was probably allowed inside! The monstrous ecclesiastical covering certainly preserves the site from the destructive weight of piety and pilgrimage, but it hardly helps our interpretative understanding.

Just across the street is another much more handsome survival, probably the most famous synagogue of all. This must have been a magnificent building, expensively built of brilliant white limestone, and in splendid contrast to the black stone of the houses around. Although it has been extensively and somewhat imaginatively reconstructed, its rich decoration gives it an undeniable aura of fine quality. Its design clearly shows that Christians should not understand ancient synagogues as a kind of Jewish local church, but rather as a school, assembly hall, or community centre. The ancillary rooms might have accommodated the *Beth Sepher* (like a primary school), the *Beth Talmud* (like a middle school), and even the *Beth Midrash* (like secondary schooling and continuing education). This was not a synagogue Jesus attended, as it cannot have been constructed before the fourth century, but it may have been built on the base of an earlier synagogue. The importance of this building is its intriguing proximity to the Christian basilica. It seems likely that both buildings were enlarged at about the same time, suggesting that Jewish and Christian communities were once able to coexist peaceably side by side within the same relatively small community. Sadly this remains debatable, as there are no records of such early ecumenical endeavour. To me, it is a subject for much hope and prayer, as we painfully relearn the lessons of religious history! The Franciscans now enclose the whole site behind fences, a ticket kiosk, and boundaries of religious convention. On entry, the sign at the gate proclaims "No Shorts"; precisely what first century fishermen would have worn!

It is utterly fascinating to feel that wandering in these ruins of ancient Capernaum is to be where Jesus once was, to sense that he lodged in some tiny house hereabouts, spoke with ordinary people busy at their work in these narrow streets, taught in a synagogue

Right: The curators of the synagogue and basilica at Capernaum expect respect.

*Above: Mount Hermon seen
across the Sea of Galilee.*

here, walked by the sea, visited Peter's mother-in-law, and sometimes took off in a boat to get away from it all. More significantly, it is also possible, perhaps, to glimpse something of precisely *what* Jesus was doing in historical and religious terms. Again, the form of piety represented in Whittier's famous hymn leads us astray. Why did Jesus get embroiled in such bitter controversy, if his message was only about a "Sabbath rest by Galilee", contemplating the "calm of hills above"? In fact, any reading of the Gospels suggests that Capernaum and the surrounding district was the scene of his most intense debates and conflicts on the sharpest issues of his time. The theology of Jesus has always been a controversial subject, for the kingdom of God is everywhere bound to be pitted against alternative orders. As a Galilean teacher of the Torah, Jesus was probably involved in the development of "northern" teaching considered by the "southern" Jerusalem school as heretical. Many scholars have come in recent years to recognise Jesus as a typical midrashic teacher (*midrash* means "seeking"), developing the implications of the written text into an "oral" teaching, which would eventually come to be written up in the Mishnah, but which in his own time threatened the status quo, dependent as it was on the written (and fixed) text.

Jesus is often depicted in sharp conflict with the local Pharisees. What is sometimes not recognised is that these arguments were something like internal party disputes; Jesus must have been very close to the Pharisees in most respects. For example, there seems to have been a consensus within Galilean Judaism that healing was allowed on the Sabbath – only the ultra-orthodox disallowed it. People flocked to hear Jesus dispute with other teachers on this and other current religious and social issues, and were often held spellbound, or speechless, by the powerful directness of his method. At other times, people were often

Above: Holidaymakers flock to Tiberias, which is sandwiched between the lake shore and steep hills.

shocked and scandalised by the way he pointed the finger, and the allusiveness of his parabolic style. Pharisees and Sadducees were at the farthest opposite poles of first century Judaism; indeed, they represented almost two completely different faiths, Temple Judaism and Torah Judaism. Jesus' journey from Galilee to Jerusalem was also a religious journey from Torah to Temple religion. Jesus was interpreting the Torah by his life, moving far beyond the fixed, fossilised conventions of textual rigidity. That exactly similar polarities, centring on divergent methods of scriptural exegesis and interpretation, have developed widely within the western churches of our own time is hardly open to doubt.

MOUNT TABOR

Lunch, during an hour's leisurely trip across the lake to Tiberias, always consists of St. Peter's fish, a tasty and palatable meal. Most people find this a most moving experience, sailing across the inland sea around which the teaching and healing ministry of Jesus was largely concentrated. It is a beautiful scene, the green hills and Tiberias to the west, the steep cliffs of the Golan range to the east glowing orange in the afternoon sun, and then, most glorious of all as the boat moves out into the lake, the best view yet of Mount Hermon, the "sheikh", wearing for most of the year his white kefiyeh of snow. It is said that the squalls made famous by the story of the stilling of the storm in Matthew 8 are quite common. Less often realised is that the episode parallels Psalm 89; verses 10-12 describe the storm in a setting between Hermon and Tabor, north and south of the lake, and verse 25 speaks of God's ultimate control. It is as though Matthew's story is a com-

mentary, or Jesus' actions are a living midrash, on the biblical text.

Tiberias has a busy shoreline with holidaymakers and tourist trappings of every description. Herod Antipas, tetrarch of Galilee, moved his capital here from Sepphoris in 18AD, and named it after the then Emperor. It has long been a Jewish centre, and today stretches for miles into the steep hills behind the town. The Haifa road climbs steeply, following a route south-west towards Mount Tabor.

Every visitor to the Holy Land afterwards relates the hair-raising twisting taxi ride to the summit of the mountain in the fleets of gleaming white stretched Mercedes operated by kamikaze drivers. This excitement perhaps detracts from one's sense of the place as the sacred site it has been considered to be from the earliest times. It has also been used as a strategic military site, as not a few biblical texts make clear. But it is hardly surprising that Christians at least from Byzantine times began to associate this perfectly formed physical feature with the transfiguration of Jesus, and this is its importance today. The view from the summit is quite wonderful, although the Barluzzi-designed basilica built on the summit in 1924 is rather less so. Just beyond the piazza of the new church is a small ruined chapel from an earlier Benedictine monastery, and here we sat to read and ponder the transfiguration narrative. Although the western church did not celebrate this gospel episode until the nineteenth century, it has always been a central festival for Eastern Orthodoxy and fundamental to Eastern understanding because it combines so many

Below: Cats of Tiberias looking for their next meal.

powerful themes. The Son shines with the uncreated light of the Father's glory, and the voice of the Spirit proclaims Christ's sonship – so it is seen as a feast of God the Trinity. Newly appointed icon painters make this their first icon. In the traditional composition, golden lines emanate from Christ towards each of the disciples, who are literally "bowled over" by their participation in the divine glory. Icons seem to capture the essence of the matter often missing in the more literalist interpretations common in the West (as exemplified in the basilica). Unless we are somehow caught up by and involved in the sacred stories, they easily pass us by unaffected. A text that won the "Hymn for Britain" TV competition in 1968, was read as a meditation:

Once on a mountain top there stood three startled men;
They watched the wheels of nature stop, and heaven break in.
Their friend of every day, the face they knew for his,
They saw, for one half hour, the way He always is.

Yet many lived and died who found of him no trace.
"Thou art a God", (the prophet cried) "who hidest thy face."
The earth lies all explored, the heavens are ours to climb,
And still no man has seen his God, at any time.

And minds that learn to scan creation like a book
Know nothing lives outside their plan, so never look.
O Lord of hidden light, forgive us who despise
The things which lie beyond our sight. And give us eyes.

The guidebook invites a visit to the Greek Orthodox monastery nearby, which can be seen over a stone wall. The wall, it is said, "highlights the character of the relationship between Catholics and Orthodox here", and there is certainly no gate in it, so undeterred we take a long walk round to the front entrance, and knock loudly on the huge iron doors. Eventually, and after much knocking, a Greek monk puts his head over the high wall, and informs us, "It is a feast; we are closed". A curious way to celebrate the festival of the Dormition of Mary, the feast in question. They were certainly keeping it in the family!

THE TURNING POINT

Walking down the mountain gave me time to think. Small lizards kept darting off the road ahead of our steps. Luke's version of the transfiguration (in chapter 9) is perhaps the most interesting, with its reference to the cloud of divine presence, and to Jesus' departure (in Greek, exodus) from Galilee. This is the turning point of Jesus' ministry, when he began to set his face towards his destiny in Jerusalem. The word used at this point by Luke implies an interior sense of direction also. It does not take very long to reach Jerusalem from here, but it could take a lifetime, and maybe forever. The Exodus theme is not far away. But where Matthew emphasises an understanding of Jesus as a new kind of Moses, Luke emphasises the travelling Jesus, always moving forward, never putting down roots, constantly on the move. This crucial decision to make this journey affects all our lives too.

This meditation brings our journey to a turning point of its own. Our aim in making this journey is to draw closer in understanding and in actual living to this person who made so much difference to people, then and since. In following the steps, not only of Jesus, but also of other disciples, pilgrims and scholars, we come to see more clearly what other generations have made of this man. We have a responsibility also, not only to our-selves but also to our own generation, to make of his story whatever is meaningful in our own context and period. The purpose of our trip is not just to follow where other people have gone, but to follow in such a way that we can also lead. This requires us to draw on the links between the Hebrew and Christian scriptures in ways that will resonate with the

Below: One inhabitant of Tabor unmoved by questions of faith, or conflict.

great themes of our own time. This task of biblical reflection comes into sharper focus as we begin to look towards Jerusalem. In one way or another, both the New Testament narrative of Jesus, and the longer, wider story of the people of God in which it is set, share the same climax, the "entry to Jerusalem".

Our journey from the desert to Galilee to Jerusalem echoes the structural design of the shortest Gospel, that of Mark. The other gospels develop and elaborate this simple, single schema. Mark begins his narrative at the great divide, the River Jordan, the boundary of the promised land, in which Jesus is baptised with words which are unmistakably already pointing to his eventual anointing as king in Jerusalem ("You are my Son" in Mark 1:11 is a quotation from Psalm 2:7, in which the Davidic regime in Jerusalem receives divine assent). The underlying question in the narrative is whether the kingship of Jesus will be recognised there, and what form it will take.

The sun set splendidly on the hills as we returned to Nazareth. It gets dark quite rapidly. As we entered Nazareth, now quite late, the sky exploded with fireworks. We asked the barman serving our drinks what it was all about. "For Our Lady", he said. Of course.

If the desert experience was one of physical discomfort, the Galilee experience has equalled it in mental discomfort. Late tonight, we had an unexpected visit from Bishop Riah, Anglican Bishop in Jerusalem, who was formerly the parish priest here in Nazareth.

Right: The millennia collide.

Why, he demanded, was he not informed of our coming? He had something to say to all Christian visitors from the West. We were aware, were we not, of the poverty, the cramped conditions and the political hopelessness of the Palestinian people? Were we to be just visitors, gazing at other people's problems from our secluded, sheltered and air-conditioned lives? If we needed a challenge to send us on our way more reflectively, this

Below: Fireworks over Nazareth. Questions and contradictions crowd in.

was it. Unable to sleep, I reflected that between Tabor and that other mountain, Calvary, Jesus stopped for one thing only. Prayer was the only stable element in an otherwise fast-moving drama. As TS Eliot puts in - though in a quite different context:

If you came this way
Taking any route, starting from anywhere,
At any time or at any season,
It would always be the same: you would have to put off
Sense and notion. You are not here to verify,
Instruct yourself, or inform curiosity
Or carry report. You are here to kneel
Where prayer has been valid.

Here, the intersection of the timeless moment
Is England and nowhere. Never and always.

Our task is to make this land the temporary context for our own journey of prayer, knowing that it is also the permanent context for our fellow Palestinian Christians.

Chapter Twelve

GOING UP TO JERUSALEM

After the transfiguration incident in Luke's gospel, Jesus "resolutely sets his face towards Jerusalem", and a long travel narrative follows. A long journey also for us today, following the coastal route south from Galilee, going west out of Nazareth in the direction of Haifa, crossing the Jezreel valley and up into the attractive limestone hills. The thin soil here supports a profusion of plants, especially anemones, in white, yellow and red. Driving along the ridge, which offers a strikingly beautiful view of the surrounding country from about 1,300 ft, we reached the traditional site of Elijah's showdown with the prophets of Baal, el-Muhraqa, the place of sacrifice. Booklets on sale seek to prove conclusively that this part of Mount Carmel accords with the details in 1 Kings 18. However, it is the theme, rather than the place, of sacrifice that seems unavoidable, as we enjoyed the glorious view over this still disputed territory. We spent some time for reflection in the chapel of the Carmelite monastery. Even the building has its story, its stones being reused after a history of destruction by Turks, Crusaders and others, and hinting at the megalithic stone circle which might once have provided Elijah with the materials for his altar. Ours is the continuation of a very old story.

Farther south along the coastal Haifa-Tel Aviv highway are the seaward slopes of the Carmel range, covered with expensive villas. The site of Caesarea Maritima is a curious place for a port, situated as it is on a line of sand and cliffs without any natural harbour or inlet. Yet it was from Caesarea that Paul sailed to Rome, after being sent here from Jerusalem under guard for trial before successive governors, Felix and Festus, and Herod Agrippa (Acts 23-27). Herod the Great had built a magnificent Roman city here, dedicated to his Roman patron Augustus Caesar, and the foundations of a remarkable artificial breakwater can still be seen. We made our way to the restored ampitheatre, where we performed an impromptu playlet, to the huge amusement of passing tourists. Dressed in blanket and turban, and with wrists bound with a chain someone produced from a nearby broken lavatory, I played the imprisoned Paul arguing the case for Christianity before Agrippa, with a script from Acts 26. One lucky student was given the part of Festus, and delivered with huge conviction the immortal line beloved of theological students everywhere: "Paul, you are raving; too much study is driving you mad" (Acts 26:24).

PONTIUS PILATE

At the modern entrance to the ampitheatre site stands a replica of a stone inscription found here, recording a dedication made by the then Roman governor, Pontius Pilate. Rome had taken direct control of Palestine in 6AD, and made Caesarea the capital and official residence. It subsequently became important as a Roman colony, a centre of Jewish rabbinic scholarship, a Christian bishopric and Byzantine city, and a place of terrible slaughter as Crusaders briefly took it from the Arabs in the twelfth century.

It was here that I noticed also a small statue of a shepherd, representing a young beardless figure with a lamb around his shoulders. This was a classical motif, applied by the first Christians to Jesus. The earliest known representation of Jesus is as a seated teacher holding an open book. Unfortunately no example has been found in Caesarea, although this was also the city in which the great Christian teacher Origen lived for 20 years (230-250)

Below: Ruins from Herod's time give a glimpse of Caesarea Maritima as it was when Paul sailed for Rome.

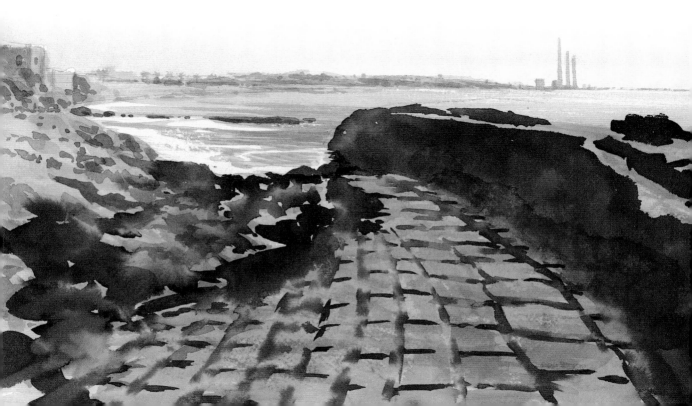

and founded a library second only in importance in the Christian world to Alexandria. However, the next earliest motif used for Christ was this image of the classical, rather than Jewish, shepherd. All the great Hebrew leaders and teachers had been shepherds (eg Moses). By such devices, the earliest Christians came to understand the meaning of Jesus the Jewish Messiah in terms of their own prevailing classical culture. Our contemporary task is exactly the same, of discovering how this story resonates with our own. The biblical text is situated historically and culturally in this particular place and period, but the stories it tells have not stood still as successive generations of Christians have lived them out in their own times and places.

Above: Echoes from long-gone conquerors reverberate along these shores.

We enjoyed lunch on the beach, sitting in the shadow of Herod's remarkable aqueduct, which remains for half its original length along the shore of the sparkling Mediterranean. The site of the nearby hippodrome is nothing but a field, although it is still possible to sense the impressive scale of the races once held here, perhaps like Ben-Hur's chariot race?

WAY OF THE SEA

South again, past Netanya, is what at first seems an unlikely site, the ruins of a Turkish fort at Antipatris or Aphek. Yet in an overgrown field behind the fort, in the undergrowth, are the surviving flagstones of a first century paved road. When Paul was brought here from Jerusalem to stay overnight on his way to Caesarea (Acts 23:23), his guards' horses' hoofs may have clattered over these very stones! Antipatris lay on the main road from Jerusalem to the sea, at the crossroads with the great north-south trade route, the Via Maris, or Way of the Sea, and was a strategic site long before Herod the Great renamed the place in honour of his father. It was from here, at Aphek, that two major battles were fought between the two peoples moving into the land of the Canaanites around the same period, from the twelfth century BC onwards. The Philistines were an advanced civilisation, already using iron and possessing building skills, coming from the sea, while the Hebrews were a relatively uncivilised, nomadic people. It was not the indigenous Canaanites who proved to be Israel's chief enemy, but rather the army of the Philistines. 1Samuel 4 & 29 tell of Israel's defeat by Philistine armies camped at Aphek, battles which firmly established the territory of Philistines in the coastal plain. The Israelites were forced to move back into the hills, and to consolidate their own emerging state around Jerusalem on much higher ground. There is surely much more to learn of how the Hebrew people long ago coexisted with their neighbours in the same land.

Above: A young shepherd carrying a lamb, an image that was also applied to Jesus.

So we too began the ascent to the holy city. The dual carriageway climbs several thousand feet before reaching the sprawling suburbs of west Jerusalem. The Philistines have gone, but their counterparts are still here, many of whom trace their origins back beyond the Roman renaming of Philistia as Palestina. It is tempting to connect "Philistine" with "Palestinian" in this way; certainly the latter have been in the land for centuries. Most Israelis have emigrated from Europe, North America and Russia within the last 50 years, and their new settlements mark the hill country for miles around.

We drove round the outskirts of the new city, so that we could begin our exploration of Jerusalem from the east, following the movements of Jesus as narrated in the gospels. Passing Mount Scopus and the Hebrew University, we made our way to the Mount of Olives, and so came to Bethany, on the Jericho road. If this is the same place as the Bethany mentioned in the gospels, it is where Jesus' *friends* lived – and stayed, unlike his *disciples*, who remained with the Teacher. The disciples are sometimes represented as uncomprehending followers, while the friends are credited (at least in John 11) with a deeper level of theological reflection. Further confirmation that literal journeys are not essential to the Christian way. Luke's travel narrative makes only passing reference to the place. Interestingly, the narrative structure of John's gospel is quite different from that of the others. There is little interest in Galilee – 80% of John's story takes place in Jerusalem, compared to only 30% in Matthew. Our own journey has been a following in the footsteps of the Jesus of the synoptic gospels, rather than the different itinerary of the fourth gospel.

The difficulties of finding a way through the different gospels seemed mirrored in a monstrous traffic jam as everyone refused to give way and just sat on their horns. Bethany is a dusty, unkempt town in the West Bank. Its Arabic name *El-Azariyeh* preserves its identification as the place where Jesus raised his friend Lazarus from the dead, the name by which it has been known since the first Christian pilgrims came here. Muslims, who also venerated the site, for centuries allowed Christians to come here freely. Alas, this is no longer the case, and the tomb of Lazarus is only accessible through the mosque, or via a narrow entrance further up the hill. The modern Franciscan church, built over the remains of earlier structures, preserves some masonry and mosaic flooring from the earliest Christian building here.

Below: For hundreds of years, believers have made their way to the Tomb of Lazarus.

The Spanish nun, Egeria, came here between 381 and 383, and writes in her travel diary of that first church and the crowds of worshippers who attended it. She was among the first wave of pilgrims who came seeking "the very place", anxious to read and understand the scriptures in their place of origin. Yet for 250 years Christianity had grown and flourished across the entire Mediterranean region without asking the question "where did it happen?" and had proclaimed the scriptures without finding any need to examine their historical context. It was only in the great renewal of the church after the conversion of Constantine in 325 that Christians began to show a fascination for the historical sites and their exact identification. It must have been bound up with the new imperial rapprochement with Christianity, and with Christianity's willingness to accommodate itself to the political order. This caused a crucial change in the church's fortunes; some argue that it marked a crucial departure from genuine, radical faith. It certainly left a rich artistic heritage, and the historical (and therefore essentially worldly) questions are still very much alive for modern Christians.

Visiting the sites, the places where events are claimed to have happened, does seem to be the main reason why pilgrims still arrive here. Perhaps the difference between a tourist and a pilgrim lies between sight and insight. Tourists want to grasp thousands of years of history and culture in moments, before moving on to the next "sight". Genuine pilgrims, on the other hand, take longer to look, think and focus, because the exterior and interior journeys are always related. This is the value of spending time in the desert (where there are no "sites") before coming here.

The street outside the tomb entrance, filled with crowds of insistent young Palestinians touting for custom, is a reminder that one suggested meaning of "Bethany" is "house of misery", and such is indeed the lot of many people living here. One feels sad and guilty, sweeping by it all in an air-conditioned coach. Genuine pilgrimage must at least encounter the contemporary experience of those who inhabit the Holy Land. But today we drove on, through Bethphage. From the road running along the ridge of the Mount of Olives, we enjoyed, for the first time, the magnificent views over the Old City in the light of the setting sun. The first glimpse of this most famous and panoramic of all religious sites stirs the emotions and the memories. The many-faceted face of this very special place is both splendid and sordid. Having arrived at this spot through the deprivation of the West Bank communities, we notice rising beyond the towers and domes of old Jerusalem the high-rise hotels and office blocks of the new city – a very different world. Planning regulations under the British Mandate limited the height of new developments until recently, and insisted upon the use of local limestone for the facades of all new buildings. The hue of the stone changes according to the light. Exploring it all must wait for another day, and we make our way in the darkness to our accommodation at St. George's College, in the compound of the Anglican Cathedral. It is oddly familiar after our Holy Land journey, this English ecclesiastical building style, but it is so out of context!

Above: Pilgrim fashion note.

__Below:__ Approaching Jerusalem. Will this be the key to our journey?

Chapter Thirteen

JERUSALEM, JERUSALEM

Early on a brilliant morning, the sun reflects powerfully from the pure white stone of the Anglican Cathedral and its surrounds. We attended an equally bright and sunny Eucharist celebrated by the Anglican Bishop in Jerusalem, every inch the local sheikh. His booming voice and unaffected intercessions lifted the soul. For the first time, at the liturgical greeting of Peace, we greeted our fellow guests at the College, from all parts of the world. The liturgy is almost identical to one used in the Church of England, with the poignant addition in the eucharistic prayer "born in Bethlehem, … died here in Jerusalem". After the service we shared a wonderful breakfast of eggs, cheeses and salads, with the inevitable humous.

From Mount Scopus, at the northern end of the Mount of Olives ridge, as its name implies, almost the whole city can be seen. As Jesus came in sight of the city (Luke 19:41) he could view the glorious panorama of city and Temple from a critical distance, and ask his disciples to see it all from his perspective. He wept over it. It was the place where opposition to Jesus' mission was at its fiercest, and in a startling image Jesus longed to take its people under his own protection as a true mother (Matthew 23:37). Perhaps he could foresee how, forty years later, Titus and his Roman legions would view this same commanding outlook, the city and its resplendent Temple they had come to destroy. Today the golden dome of *Haram esh-Sharif*, the noble sanctuary, glistens from the site of that long-vanished Temple, and provides for all modern travellers a visual focus for their exploration of this superbly beautiful but immensely frustrating city.

As our guide began to help us make some geographical and historical sense of this wide

Right: The Anglican Cathedral in Jerusalem, like a piece of rural England transported over a continent.

82

Right: Sometimes the signs are necessary in this city of turmoil.

vista spread out below us, the contemporary realities of life also impressed themselves on us. Young Palestinians tried to sell us films, postcards and camel rides. Young Israeli soldiers of both sexes, heavily armed, stood in groups everywhere. Behind us, and just across the road, it seems, the city ends and the desert begins, such is the abrupt change in rainfall beyond this ridge. Jerusalem lies on the dividing line between fruitfulness and wilderness; the old Roman road down to Jericho can be faintly traced on the distant landscape. The city occupies a site that is not well defended, and stands lower than the surrounding hills. The size and location of the walled city have changed often, and the present line of the ramparts dates largely from the sixteenth century.

The ancient city established by David in the tenth century BC now lies outside and to the south of these much later walls, near the only water source, the Gihon spring. This is to be the starting point of our journey through the city, and through some of its immense and bewildering history, and its significance for so many contemporary believers. Since David's time, when the city was very small, it has exercised a hold on people's imagination and faith that is hardly consistent with its insignificant physical and geographical position. This ancient and modern city remains firmly at the centre of global international relations, inspiring both political controversy and religious passion with equal intensity. It is not a peaceful place. For so many it remains a potent symbol of the age-long

Right: Pet cockerel at Dominus flevit — where else but here?

Above: *One way traffic in Gethsemane.*

desire for peace on earth, even while its present reality is a place of blind hatreds and deep discord. Occupying the north-south limestone ridge forming the backbone of the Holy Land, it stands at the heart of several religious worlds. It straddles a watershed in more ways than one. A Canaanite holy city of the Jebusite tribe long before David captured it, it has always been what it still is, a multi-dimensional place of pilgrimage, real and imaginary. Its name probably relates to some Canaanite deity ("the foundation of the god Shalem"?) or even to some more primitive deity known in Mesopotamia and Egypt to be associated with sunset. If this is the case, then the notion of the ending or completion of the day is contained in the root meaning of *shalom/salaam*, wholeness, completeness, and therefore "peace". In Hebrew it takes the form of a dual noun (a special plural form applied only to things found in pairs) which suggests a special kind of place between several cultures, just as it is physically situated between two climates and two valleys. Muslims know the city as "The Holy", *al-Quds*, from where Mohammed ascended to heaven.

On the Mount of Olives, there is precious little left of the two basilicas which once rivalled the Church of the Holy Sepulchre in importance during the earliest period of Christian occupation. We walked down a walled path to the modern church of Dominus Flevit. Touchingly, a friar seemed to converse with a resident rooster outside the church

Above: Monastic life carries on, regardless of the daily flood of visitors.

of Jesus' tears. A Jewish funeral was taking place in the huge cemetery that occupies much of the hillside. Forlorn and desecrated during the Jordanian occupation, but now neat and well ordered, every tomb bearing a stone. This echoes the ancient Bedouin practice of raising a heap of stones over burial plots, a reminder of the desert origins of the Jewish people. A little below, the seven cupolas of the Russian Church of St. Mary Magdalene add to the eclectic Christian presence here. Churches of all traditions have long sought to maintain a foothold in the land where their faith was born. These interests often overlapped with national policy, as many European states sought to gain influence in this vital East-West frontier region.

At the foot of the hill lies the garden of Gethsemane. The few remaining olive trees which give the place its name now serve as posts for the "one way only" signs that guide visitors through this small space to the dark interior of the modern Church of All Nations. The crush of visitors does little to allow the building to resonate with its theme. A lovely motif of birds with a chalice over a running crown of thorns surrounds the rock before the altar. Notices outside repeat a warning: "No explanations in the church". A warning to theologians, perhaps, as well as tour guides! The gospel demands not to be explained but experienced. The Tomb of the Virgin Mary, close by, is a very early site, even if the doctrine associated with it is not. Through a Crusader-period arch, steps lead down into an

Below: First century Jewish tombs.

underground church of some size, hung with many lamps and icons of various traditions. Its chequered history means that all the Eastern churches now worship here. So a candle, bought from a Greek monk, is taken into the edicule (meaning "small building") guarded by a Coptic monk, containing the altar of the tomb in which it is believed Mary was laid. These beliefs are also held in the Muslim tradition, as is indicated by the small *miqrab* nearby.

KIDRON WADI

Separating the Mount of Olives from the old city is the Kidron wadi, a completely dry valley containing many old tombs and monuments carved directly from the rock, some dating from the first century BC. The ancient spring is now enclosed, like much else in this land of holy sites, beneath grottoes of various dates and faiths. The walls of the old city rise precipitously above a path across the valley bottom.

Above: Warren's shaft.

Facing the Jewish graves on the Mount of Olives is an Islamic cemetery situated on the steep slope below the walls. Both faiths expect the final days to be inaugurated from this Kidron valley. From Gethsemane we saw a Muslim funeral procession emerge from the Lion Gate, the plain wooden coffin preceded by a man carrying a long branch of palm. Of course this was an instant reminder to us of the gospel narrative of Jesus' entry into Jerusalem by donkey, recalled each year on "Palm" Sunday. Palms are widely associated with victory, which explains their use at funerals, and why they were taken up later as Christian symbols of the triumph of the cross of Christ. But the stories recounted in the three synoptic gospels do not mention palm branches, just trees and greenery in general. It is possible that the original setting of the gospel story may be the Jewish festival of Tabernacles, during which branches of myrtle are waved, part of a primitive rain ritual. The waving of branches simulates the wind that brings the rain, and therefore the crops. And the crops guarantee salvation for another year, which explains the age-old connection in religion between the seasons of the year, the renewal of life, and the promise of life after death. Jerusalem is full of Christian holy sites, established here many centuries after the time of Jesus, so it is a challenge to imagine Jesus in his original Jewish setting.

Across the Kidron is the site of the original settlement known as the City of David. The steep slope of Mount Ophel leads to recent excavations revealing several layers of ancient habitation. Some stepped supports of dry stone wall terracing on the side of the slope have been dated to the Jebusite/Canaanite period, possibly to be identified with the *Millo*, which David is said to have built up and enclosed after capturing the city (1 Samuel 5:9). "Warren's shaft" leads to the tunnel constructed at a later date during Hezekiah's reign when Assyria threatened to attack the city (2 Chronicles 32). This earliest settlement now lies outside the present walls, just below the Temple Mount. It was built on the ridge between the two converging valleys of Kidron on the east and Tyropoeon on the west, which meant that its further development was towards the north, and uphill. This is where Solomon began to build the first Temple, to which worshippers from the city literally "went up", a phrase so often used to describe worship there, and echoed in the Psalms of Ascent, 120-134.

Climbing farther to the modern road skirting the walls at this point brought us to yet more recent excavations on the south side of the Temple Mount. Here more than fifteen *miqva'oth* have been discovered, one clearly seen with a double stair. The stone steps (some preserving original Herodian period stones) once led to the imposing southern double gate, and were apparently used for teaching purposes. Certainly Jesus taught here ("Master", the disciples said as they were leaving the Temple, "look at these huge stones, these fine buildings...." Mark 13:2) and Mary's purification must surely have included ritual washing in the *miqveh*.

The Herodian stonework retains a quality and scale all its own. The so-called Robinson's Arch, the massive springs of which can still be seen, was the largest in the world at the time. It led from the street into the sheer face of the Temple retaining wall, the lower courses of which survive, enormous bossed stone blocks each weighing up to a hundred tons. The street was far below the modern level, and the towering height of the wall must have seemed incredible and monumental. Even the remaining stones are impressive. There are still points at which the Hasmonean and Herodian stonework can be distinguished.

Below: Hasidic cats look as smart as their owners.

Hasmonean rule brought a measure of Jewish independence, and some reality was given to all the ancient hopes and dreams of the Jewish people. Jerusalem acquired a mystical status, and Ezekiel's vision during the exile in Babylon was given some concrete form. He pictured it (Ezekiel 5:5, 38:12) as a cosmic mountain, the place where heaven and earth meet, and down which flowed rivers that watered the entire earth. Ancient ideas about the centre of the earth became attached to Jerusalem. Here began that theological geography which insisted that all the great events in history occurred here, and which no doubt provided the impetus for Herod to reconstruct the Temple in the magnificent manner which his political ambitions demanded.

Earlier theologies had understood the land and the city as gifts from God. Yet the land had to be conquered and taken from other peoples. This awkward dilemma lives on in still-unresolved conflict. Much of this stretch of western wall now forms the backdrop to an expansive new plaza, built after the Arab homes in the area had been bulldozed away only days after the capture of East Jerusalem in the six-day war of 1967. Our bags were thoroughly searched at the military barriers, and the whole area had an intensive army presence. I found it difficult to join in the prayers being offered here. Do those Jews praying today at the temple wall for the restoration of their vision really weigh the potential cost? They are only the latest in a long line of those who have sought to root their identity and security here in this city. It was a

tradition eagerly appropriated by Christians once the city became their domain. Naturally, future events came to be expected in the same place also - the Resurrection, and the final day. Much contemporary Christian interest in the future of Jerusalem echoes this potentially tragic legacy. Nothing in its history has saved this city from catastrophe. After 135AD, a final and much longer Jewish exile began. Centuries of longing for return gave birth in the nineteenth century to Zionism, and these ancient themes powerfully supported the search for a modern Jewish homeland. It might have been elsewhere, but the old longing proved too strong, with the well-known tragic consequences.

Despite all the talks, peace processes and a new Palestinian authority in parts of the occupied territories, nothing seems to have changed in recent years. As we walked back to the College through the dark, crowded alleys of the old city, squads of Israeli soldiers look on as menacingly as ever, and life and business struggle to survive in these unkempt, noisy, bustling thoroughfares.

Left: After centuries of exile, Jews are able to return to their modern homeland.

Below: Praying at the western wall.

Above: Looking out over Arab East Jerusalem.

Chapter Fourteen

ROCKS, STONES AND QUARRIES

ere in Arab East Jerusalem, life wakes to a cacophony of sound – the call to prayer from mosques close by, the heavy roar of passing traffic and the constant blaring of horns, punctuated by the occasional strange-sounding blast from army jeeps and police car sirens. Behind high wired compounds, stand the Israeli Law Courts and the Ministry of Justice.

A wonderful view of the old city, and a microcosmic sense of its depth of history and its underlying tensions and contradictions, can be gained simply by walking around the medieval ramparts. The Damascus gate occupies the site of the main entrance to the pagan Roman city of Aelia Capitolina, so called by the Emperor Hadrian after its complete destruction following the Bar Kochba rebellion of 135AD. An Israeli soldier, machine gun at the ready, dangles his legs through an opening high in the facade, while people jostle in the crowded street below, milling along Salah-e-Din Street, waiting for friends or buses, gathering in groups to talk, selling foodstuffs for the local Arab population, and touting all manner of tourist items. Local people move through this noisy, boisterous setting with its pungent mixture of exotic smells, some sickly, some more appetising, towards the Dome of the Rock, a golden spectacle gleaming through a maze of rooftop television antennae. Friday prayers at the el-Aqsa mosque draw very large crowds of worshippers.

The city walls enclose four quarters, different worlds still physically separated from each other in such a tiny space. The Muslim quarter is huddled and poor, with much of its architectural heritage derelict. Alongside ancient housing in dark winding alleys stand handsome Mameluke palaces, their red, white and black stone banding sadly decayed, and occupied mostly by squatters. Gates and lintels are carved with stars, not of David, but of Solomon, believed by Muslims to be not only wise but magical. A lost world, neglected, one suspects, for more than economic reasons.

Westwards, these huddled rooftops and courtyards give way to the equally congested Christian quarter, with the grey domes of the Church of the Resurrection and the tower of the Lutheran Church visible at its heart. Turning south at the north-west corner, there is a break in the wall at the Jaffa gate, an opening made in 1898 to enable the German Kaiser, Wilhelm II, to enter the city on horseback during his state visit, when the Lutheran Church was opened. An act not without profound overtones; General Allenby, when he entered Jerusalem in 1917, did not make the same mistake, but dismounted before entering.

Exploring this immediate area began with a coffee at Christ Church. This was the first Anglican church in the Holy Land, built to serve the growing community of British diplomats and others who came here in the nineteenth century to open up trade and influence in the Middle East. Today it describes itself as Protestant, and seems dedicated primarily to converting Jews to Christianity. Nearby stands the Citadel, where Herod the Great's palace once stood. There is a good museum documenting the troubled history of the city. A group of young Israeli army conscripts were being given an educational tour. The same

Below: At the Damascus Gate.

Above: Butchers shop in the Suq.

bored expression on young faces suggested that the military heroes of previous generations have been displaced by the international celebrities who dominate youth culture the world over. I found it somewhat disturbing that this army of occupation needed educating in its own cause. What do those young Israelis make of the Armenian quarter, just a short distance from here? It is an enclosure within an enclosure. Armenia is a people without a state, but their national experience of holocaust (two million people were massacred by Turkish forces in 1915) defines their tenacious identity just as the Shoah justifies the existence of the Israeli Jewish state. The Armenian Cathedral of St. James with its seminary and patriarchate is one of the oldest-established in the city.

EXPANSION

Back on the ramparts, the outlook to the west includes the first expansion of the city beyond the old walls, one of many developments financed by the most famous British Jew, the philanthropist Sir Moses Montefiore. Once on the dangerous border with Jordan, it has become since 1967 a chic, exclusive neighbourhood with a restored windmill as a memorial to its founder. Turning the south-west corner, the various buildings on Mt. Zion come into view, housing the traditional sites of David's supposed tomb and the Room of the Last Supper. The location of the original Mount Zion is open to question. The ancient church on this site, Hagia Zion, was destroyed by the Persians in 614. What is today called the "Upper Room" is a magnificent example of Crusader architecture, later furnished with a miqrab and renovated Ottoman windows. The quality both of light and acoustics are

Saladin St East Jerusalem Post office near Damascus Gate

lovely. It is heartening to find that the Israeli Ministry of Religious Affairs keeps this room open as a room of prayer for all peoples. It is built over a functioning synagogue and next to a mosque.

Leaving the ramparts at the Zion gate provides access to the Jewish quarter, rebuilt since 1967, once the poorest area and now the most prosperous. Sounds of boys from Orthodox families reciting Torah texts issued from the high windows of the many *yeshuvas* in this district. There are several excellent excavations of large mansions from the

Second Temple period with lovely artefacts, mosaics and frescoes. Columns from the Cardo Maximus, the main artery of the Byzantine city, have been carefully reconstructed. The Hurvah (or ruined) synagogue has been partially restored, adjoining a mosque which presumably no longer functions. A synagogue on this site served an Ashkenazi community since the Middle Ages. It was rebuilt in 1864, and a poignant photograph shows prayers being said here when news of the extent of the European holocaust reached Jerusalem in 1942. Another photograph shows a soldier of the Arab Legion standing in the rubble after its destruction in 1948.

We walked back across the old city to the entrance to the Dome of the Rock at the Morocco Gate. On the way we saw a group of soldiers arresting a Palestinian and taking him off into a side alley. Their rough handling of the man added to the general sense of

Above: Walking through the Old City.

Above: At our feet were the scratch marks of games played by Roman soldiers.

oppression by an occupying power. Yet this is the way it has always been here. No city has been fought over so many times as Jerusalem.

The site known in Jewish tradition as the Temple Mount covers a huge area of thirty-five acres. The sun reflected a blinding light from the white stones, as we took off our shoes and added them to the pile at the door. The light filters softly inside through glass set in intricate filigree windows, lighting the wonderful mosaics and the heavy ornamentation in blue, green and gold. In the centre is the rock, and underneath, a cave. The building is a Byzantine octagon, originally constructed soon after the surrender of the city to Caliph Omar in 638AD, and remains the third most important shrine in Islam. The el-Aqsa mosque nearby was also constructed by Christian craftsmen a hundred years later. Behind a Crusader Gothic entrance is a huge seven-aisled space (there were originally fourteen aisles), the floor covered in very fine carpets. The small Islamic museum contains remains that hint at the splendour now destroyed. In the court before the entrance stands a large Byzantine fountain – a thorough wash is necessary before prayers – a throwback to Christian baptismal practice.

The shock of turquoise and gold is dazzling when first seen. The complex non figurative patterning of the tiled walls seemed somehow obsessive however..

Officials at the Dome of the Rock seem jumpy. It is said that in recent years some well-financed fundamentalist Christian-Zionist groups have laid secret plans to blow up the Dome of the Rock, and have the materials to do so ready and hidden. This is not a story to be taken lightly: right-wing believers, Jewish and Christian, have come to believe that the Jewish Temple must be rebuilt before the final Armageddon can take place. In such a volatile place, such threat of destruction is a frighteningly real possibility. No wonder the Israeli military guard every entrance to the site, and its keepers probably have every justification for their nervousness.

North of the Temple Mount is the start of the traditional Via Dolorosa, still followed by Christians tracing the "way of the Cross." The Antonia fortress built by Herod stood here, although the actual last journey of Jesus would have been from the Citadel rather than here. Nearby is the Ecce Homo convent of the Sisters of Zion, a French order established here in 1855 to promote understanding between Christians and Jews. Their chapel incorporates three Roman arches from the time of Hadrian, one of which continues into the street. At a lower level is a stone pavement from the same period, the Lithostrotus, containing the scratch marks for Roman soldiers' games.

Above: People watch each other in this unsettled city.

OLD CITY SHOPPING

The old city provides many shopping opportunities! In the Jewish quarter of the old city we were offered at tremendous discount a still very expensive silver Tyrian Shekel from an elderly coin dealer. He took an all-consuming interest in his subject, and conversation provided free-flowing information. These were the only coins allowed in the Jewish Temple (hence the need for moneychangers there) and were struck in Tyre, an independent district, and so carried an image of the Phoenician god-king Melkart. Syncretism seems to be present in all religious practice. A little later, only a short walk but a world away in the Christian quarter, we hit upon an enormous icon emporium, a shop which seemed to reach back for room after room, under low arches, with a huge ancient cistern. As we considered our icon purchase ("Good price for you!"), we watched a large troop of Franciscans and pilgrims wind their way singing Latin chants along the Via Dolorosa, somewhat incongruously preceded and followed by Israeli army jeeps. The occupying power keeps the peace between Christians here! Being Friday, there were many Muslim pilgrims in the city also today, and the suqs were very crowded.

At this point we set out with others of our group on our own Way of the Cross. We walked in silence together, sharing the carrying of a

Above: Muslim mother and children at the Dome of the Rock.

wooden cross, through the suqs as the shops began
to close, people started to go home, children began
to play, cats (hundreds of them, it seemed) began to
scavenge, and the light began to fade and the heat
became less intense. The whole devotion was moving and thoughtful. I was surprised to find that the
present Via Dolorosa takes a curious route through
some of the filthiest corners imaginable. Just so, the
unwary Western pilgrim coming across the Church
of the Sepulchre (as the Crusaders called it; more
properly the Church of the Resurrection) for the
first time is likely to be surprised and perhaps disappointed. Its bewildering history is echoed in the
sheer complexity of the buildings and the incredible
"status quo" by which the behaviour of its various
Christian tenants is regulated.

Is this really the site of Jesus' death? Those who
queue to touch the rock through a hole below the
Crucifixion altar seem undeterred by such unsuit-
able questions. None of the available evidence
denies the possibility of the validity of the site. The
empty tomb, of course, if that is what it was, sur-
vived only until 1009, when an untypically anti-
Christian Caliph destroyed it. On the site today
stands a hideous nineteenth century kiosk, like a
peep show. Inside this edicule, we lit a candle as a
Greek monk on a stepladder filled the many lamps

with oil. I was drawn into conversation with a Coptic
Orthodox monk watching over the small alternative shrine
that backs onto the main Greek Orthodox shrine. He told me
something of his life and faith in Egypt, a fellow Christian
from a tradition and a church very dissimilar to mine.
We blessed each other, Fr. Anthony and I, as we
parted. Groups of noisy and seemingly uncomprehending visitors were shown around this
strange and curiously empty space, or queued to
get a look inside in the edicule. At Easter, the
whole place is vibrant with the clamorous sights and

Above: Entrance to Tomb.

sounds of the various dissonant liturgies and processions. Many
hours could be spent in this most intriguing of all churches. Our most precious moment
came as we were led deep underground through the Armenian excavations into the
ancient quarry on which the church rests. Here was found, quite recently, at the level of
the first church on the site, a small outline drawing of a ship with the words *Domine ivimus*,
"Lord, we have come". Christians like us have been coming from far afield to this place for
many centuries – the drawing can be accurately dated between 326 and 335. As so often,
small things and momentary conversations are the most revealing.

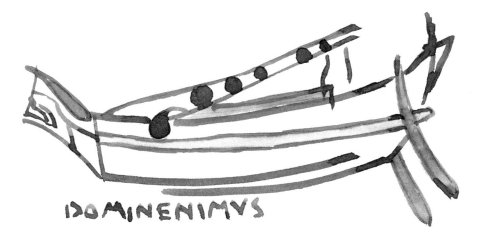

DOMINENIMVS

*Left: The earliest pilgrims
have left their tribute,
"Lord, we have come."*

SHRINE OF CHRISTENDOM

The Church of the Resurrection, as the central shrine of Christendom, is a sober reminder
of the broken world, and of the broken body set in, and not apart, from it. A place that
has accumulated so much accretion, in so many styles, given rise to so much bloodshed
and which still houses only a status quo of rival factions. One looks for majesty and finds
squalor, for a grand setting and finds dirty, cramped and narrow streets, for light and finds
dingy darkness, for peace and finds only rigidity and division.

The Dome of the Rock, the Islamic holy place built on the ruins of the Jewish Temple,
is the opposite of all these things, majestic, awe-inspiring, a perfect geometric form, a
unity of structure and purpose, a reflection of the certainty and triumph of the faith of its
builders. Too much certainty, too little ambiguity.

Lighting candles, Holy Sepulchre

Below: Christians maintain
a presence here.

The Western Wall, by contrast, is only a length of genuinely historic, if bitter, stones. A shrine, a place of hope for the future and anguish in the present. What kind of future is suggested by what is happening all round it - not just the constant praying at its foot, nor the fervent religious and nationalistic assemblies that gather here, but the opening of the plaza, swept clean and smooth, heavily policed by an ever-present security cordon, where once were ordinary houses? Jerusalem is being heavily and rapidly Judaized, not simply in the ring of illegal Jewish settlements, but here at its heart. The culture and pulse of the entire city are almost wholly Jewish. Christians are distressingly few, and still diminishing, and Muslims are confined to the lowest form of economic activity - selling to tourists. Those who come to pray here should realise what the practice of their faith costs in human terms — population displacement (there is a nastier phrase for it) and injustice. This people should know about exile! The Western Wall represents all this, perhaps, to those who see it, not as symbol of tenacious survival and a pledge of rebuilding the ancient Temple, but as a wall, a dead end, a barrier of enmity and partition (a phrase from Ephesians 2:14) and certainly not an indicator of fresh hopes for mutual respect, tolerance and dialogue.

Three centres, three faiths, each the product of history, of religious dissension, of social and cultural misunderstanding, of the urge to express dominance. Each is a piece of stony ground, part of the unyielding rock that forms the bulk of the geology of Israel. The Dome is set on its eponymous rock; the Western Wall is built of uncompromising stones; and the Church of the Resurrection is built in a rock quarry.

Retracing our steps we find, behind St. George's Cathedral on a dry and dusty pitch, two teams of Palestinian youths competing fiercely and noisily in a soccer match in the gathering darkness. A truly universal language. Half-time coincides with the call to prayer; I notice some, but not all, do obeisance.

Later, with a friend who lives in the city and works with the Palestinian Authority in Gaza, we returned to the Armenian quarter, now quiet and empty except for the lively little restaurant we visited. After a wonderful meal, walking back along the dark street, we passed a man with a machine gun slung casually over his shoulder. We took him for a security guard. No, our friend said angrily, any Israeli settler is entitled to carry such weapons in the occupied territories. But there have been several fatal stabbings recently, of Jews in the old city, and of Arabs in west Jerusalem. This beautiful and frightening city contains so many layers of hidden meaning and potential threat.

"LET HIM GO UP"

This is a city of pilgrimage to which so many people come, some to visit, some to settle, some to pray, but some to stake a claim to what has always been disputed. The books of the Hebrew Bible are collected in an order different from the Christian Bible, ending with 2 Chronicles and the proclamation of Cyrus, King of Persia: "The Lord … has charged me to build him a house at Jerusalem. To every man of his people now among you I say … *let him go up*". So the Jewish people, ever since their total expulsion from the city in 135AD, have continued to want to return to it. Some regimes down the centuries have been more tolerant of their presence than others, and superpowers continue to be involved. The words are so similar to those scratched on the rock of Golgotha by ancient Christian pilgrims, *Domine ivimus*. They did not come to stay, however.

Below: Palestinian children playing.

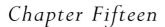

Right: You have to stoop to enter the ancient doorway in the church at Manger Square, Bethlehem.

Chapter Fifteen

BETHLEHEM TO GOLGOTHA

I woke today feeling still unsettled by the events of yesterday. I began to think that I would never make sense of this place. The frightening tensions between the faiths and races threaten to explode at any moment. The difficulty of coming to terms with such closely juxtaposed holy sites in the old city, and the surprising existential meaning we found in undertaking a simple Way of the Cross yesterday – these new realities, I realised, had quickly and powerfully submerged the other questions we had brought with us to Jerusalem. Who was, and is, Jesus, and why is he important? Thinking back to the gospel narrative, it seems at times that Jesus himself must have been swept along by the current of intrigues and events of that final week here in Jerusalem. Certainly the city has this effect. There are so many questions here, constantly on the surface, clamouring for attention, like the constant honking of the cars outside the window. Such a traffic in profound questions!

Today we carried these questions beyond the city, a few miles south to the West Bank town of Bethlehem. It is by no means a "little town" but a large Arab community with both Christian and Muslim populations and a famous university. Tourist buses usually head straight for Manger Square, and the new Palestinian Authority is constantly looking for ways of encouraging them to spend more than the average twenty minutes there. The place certainly has a longer story to tell than that told by the western Christmas carols constantly sung by one group after another in the cave grotto below the church.

The word *beth-lechem* may mean "house of meat"(or bread) but in apparent contradiction the root *lhm* could also mean "war" or "dream". In the Bible, it is not simply the place of Jesus' birth according to one tradition, but has other, deeper, associations with the fundamental theme of "journey". The town first appears in Genesis, when Rachel, Jacob's wife (whose alleged tomb we passed on the way from Jerusalem), died in childbirth on the way here from Bethel. Its name then was Ephratah, or "place of sorrow"(Genesis 35:19). Jeremiah recalls Rachel's weeping for her children... The book of Ruth tells of a journey of love all the way from Moab to Bethlehem, a love that breaks down ethnic barriers and provides a Moabite great-grandmother for the Jewish King David. In the tradition, Bethlehem represents this journey of pain and sorrow towards expectation, conception and birth. In a sense, the nativity of Jesus is already written before Luke gathers up these themes in his narrative. It is surely a story still being lived in the contemporary expectation and pain of the Palestinian people as they seek to bring their new autonomy into a constructive relationship with the surrounding Israelis.

STOOP TO ENTER

Manger Square is all that is left of the great church's original atrium. The ancient doorway of the church is so low that one must stoop to enter. Whatever the reason for that, it is a powerful reminder of the traditional liturgical bow at the *incarnatus est* in the Christian Creed, a recognition that in Jesus, God "stoops" to share human life, which is, after all, the central meaning of this shrine. Inside, the Basilica of the Nativity is a truly remarkable building, built by the Emperor Justinian in 540. Mosaics from the original building can still be seen below the present floor level, as well as equally impressive twelfth century mosaics high on the south wall. The original marble font was large enough for adult candidates. The east end is built over a cave complex, one of which is known as the cave of the Nativity, hung with candles and curtains. Set in the floor beneath a white marble altar is the famous silver star with the inscription: HIC DE VIRGINE MARIA JESUS CHRISTUS NATUS EST (Here, Jesus Christ was born of the Virgin Mary). Possibly an event transposed from elsewhere, but nevertheless recognised as "the" cave (not stable, of course they do not exist here!) from very early times. Jerome lived here, possibly in the caves, and may also have produced the Vulgate (the Bible in Latin) here. With all this in mind I listened while three Armenian monks sang their midday office in a small chapel in the southern apse.

Our party was able to celebrate a Eucharist by kind permission of the Franciscan White Sisters just around the corner of Manger Square. Their hospitality stretched to allowing a woman priest to preside, contrary to their own Roman Catholic tradition. She spoke movingly of how Christians must labour to bring to birth that which was always in the heart and mind of God. A trained midwife, she expressed the struggle for the ordination of women, after so many centuries of priesthood restricted to males, as itself a labour of bringing to birth something more of God's truth and justice. And this groundbreaking generation of women priests must also be midwives, bringing new models of ministry into the world.

On the return journey we stopped in west Jerusalem. The Holyland Hotel boasts an unusual large-scale model of the city as it is conjectured to have been laid out in the Herodian period – in other words, the city as Jesus knew it. Just a curiosity at first, it proved to hold the keys to a better understanding than I had been able to achieve standing yesterday on the actual Temple Mount. The model reveals how the Temple operated in relation to the life of the city, and how the place must have looked at festival time, especially at Passover, when many thousands of pilgrims would have been encamped outside its walls all around. Smoke from the many individual animal sacrifices must have been rising constantly from the altar. It brings sharply into focus the climax of the journey of Jesus, his confrontation with the Temple authorities, his display of anger at the stalls of the moneychangers, and the reasons for his arrest, trial and execution at Passover time. The story as recounted in the New Testament contains deliberate theological overlay, for that is the nature of the story being told. But the model explicitly reveals that the Temple, and its system of sacrifice, is at the heart of it all, both historical and theological.

OPPOSITION TO THE POLITICAL ORDER

Jesus was clearly perceived as a threat to the established order. Whether he was part of the radical opposition to the political order emerging from the desert is open to question. That his earliest followers after his death proclaimed in his name (and therefore, presumably, based on things he actually did and said) a new future in which all distinctions between races, sexes and classes would disappear is historically certain. Paul summed it up: "Baptised into union with Jesus, you have all put on Christ. There is no such thing as Jew and Greek, slave and freeman, male and female: you are all one person in Christ Jesus". (Galatians 3:28). It is odd and shaming to think that Jerusalem today, in its separate quarters, its armed hostility, its barely suppressed violence, represents almost the exact opposite of such a prospect. In this respect it is still at the world's centre, a microcosm of all that is hateful. But in ancient Jerusalem, as the model so clearly reveals, the Temple was above all else the marker of boundaries, the creator of separatisms, barriers,

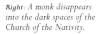

Right: A monk disappears into the dark spaces of the Church of the Nativity.

and obstructions. In the courts of the Temple, the distinctions between men and women, priest and layperson, Jew and Gentile, were absolute. Indeed, holiness was defined by the exclusion of women and Gentiles. Posted on the soreg wall between the inner and outer courts, apparently, was the following warning:

"no man of another race is to enter within the fence and enclosure around the Temple. Whoever is caught will have only himself to thank for the death which follows".

Above: The silver star which marks the supposed site of the birth of Jesus.

Subsequent Christian texts make perfectly clear the meaning of Jesus' journey, not simply to Jerusalem, but more particularly to the Temple. "Christ is our peace, Gentiles and Jews, he made the two one, and in his own body of flesh and blood has broken down the enmity which stood like a dividing wall between them". (Ephesians 2:14). Paul again says: "We are those he has called from among Jews and Gentiles alike… in the very place where they were told "You are no people of mine" they shall be called children of the living God" (Romans 9:26). This Christian truth was denied in the very stones of the Temple. Now Gentiles occupy that same Temple Mount, but sadly the enmity seems as strong as ever.

One early Christian text in particular, the letter to Jewish Christians, or Hebrews, argues most strongly for a complete break between Temple practice and Christian worship. It may have been written soon after Roman armies had in fact destroyed the Temple in 70AD. In any case this text connects most strongly with the theme of sacrifice already hinted at in our long journey. Neither the altar, the priest, nor the sacrificial victim has either physical location or religious validity any longer; the gates and walls enclosing and defining this way of communion with God are defunct. The climax of Jesus' journey, we are told, occurs "outside the gate" (Hebrews 5:12). This is precisely what the model makes clear, that the site of Golgotha, an abandoned quarry full of stone tombs, was at that time *outside* the city walls. (Today the same site, underneath the Church of the Resurrection, lies within a much later wall).

So the journey leads outwards. It moves on outside the Temple *and* the city. Unlike other reformist and revolutionary movements of the time, bent on changing or overturning the Temple system and establishment, the Jesus movement is not merely critical, but is heading in a new direction. "Here, we have no lasting city" (Hebrews 13:14). The sacrificial system and the holy city are no longer means to gaining a heavenly city, but are obstacles to it. The Christian vision of the heavenly city pointedly has no Temple at all (Revelation 21:22). The starting point for the new Jerusalem is *outside* the old one, and in a place formerly considered defiled and unholy. This is the parting of the ways. In a sense,

Above: Armenain monks singing the office: Bethlehem.

the gateway to the new Jerusalem was a journey back into the desert, leaving the old promised land behind. A centrifugal, not a centripetal journey.

With the hindsight of this journal, it now seems entirely appropriate that, just as a clearer picture of interwoven historical and theological strands was beginning to emerge, we moved on to Yad Vashem ("a place and a name"), the memorial to those millions whose places and names were extinguished during the Holocaust in central Europe. It occupies a large hilltop position, scattered with modern pieces of sculpture, including a very compelling bronze set against the skyline overlooking the site. A large exhibition hall catalogues the Nazi crimes. The empty space of the Hall of Remembrance invites our prayers and written comments. An avenue of trees is planted for the "righteous ones", Gentiles who helped Jews to escape the pogroms. The Children's Memorial, a few candles in a room of mirrors reflecting a thousand points of light, is perhaps most poignant of all. It is almost impossible to spend time here without shedding tears — tears for the victims, and tears also for those who now abuse in return. Why cannot Israelis see how the victim has become the aggressor, again bent on creating Lebensraum for itself? We left with a terrible sadness, especially as the perpetrators of so much violence, in this as in previous centuries, have called themselves Christians. Again, the theme of sacrifice comes back to haunt our journey, as it haunts all subsequent Jewish theology. Where was God? How is sacrifice an appropriate concept in such a context? Is theology any longer possible after Auschwitz? The contemporary Jewish poet, Asanath Petrie, writes:

> *You taught our father Abraham*
> *that his son need not be sacrificed.*
> *Teach us also.*
> *We bound each one of our children to this people,*
> *to this land.*
> *It is all Your altar.*
> *Teach us so that their willingness and ours,*
> *leaves them unmaimed.*
> *As whole as was Isaac and holy in Thy sight.*
> ("HOLY IN THY SIGHT". FROM: OASIS IN TIME GEFEN 1994)

The ancient and modern parallels again. Rabbi Abraham Heschl has claimed: "The state of Israel is God's answer to Auschwitz ... it enables us to bear Auschwitz without radical despair." It is an answer that goes all the way back to Masada, and Eleazar's notion of a chosen and inviolate people who choose not to survive rather than become slaves. Suicide hailed as the supreme heroism, however, is also the supreme blasphemy – that the future must be of our own making, that God can only exist on our terms. Even Eleazar must have realised that belief in an inviolable racial and religious community was a deception. Yet modern Zionist Israel has reached a similar impasse. The Palestinian enemy will not acquiesce, even though its resistance in the form of terrorism plays into Israel's hands. The locally inspired intermittent uprising, the *intifada*, however, using the weapons of David (stones!) against a heavily armed Goliath, strikes Israel at its most vulnerable point: the morality of seizing land that belongs to others, and in defiance of the international community.

I had one more visit to make. Just a stone's-throw from St. George's Cathedral, hidden behind a high wall near the East Jerusalem bus station, is the so-called Garden Tomb. It has not the slightest claim to authenticity as a possible historical site of the resurrection of Jesus, despite the best efforts of the guides there to suggest otherwise. The preserved first century tomb in the garden, however, is certainly an impressive survival, and the atmosphere more peaceful and conducive to the kind of spiritual reflection to which many western Christians are accustomed. The very fact that it is dismissed by scholars and experts may suggest that it is more likely to be the place where the real Jesus might be found, now as then, not among the religious specialists and the mainstream churches but hidden with the scorned and rejected, the sidelined and the dismissed.

Below: The very tidy "Garden Tomb"...

Right: At the checkpoint, heading into the desert again.

Chapter Sixteen

GOING DOWN TO JERICHO

This morning a chance to hear a talk by a Christian Palestinian human rights lawyer who is involved in the Middle East peace process. Having helped to draft the 1994 agreement, he is now severely disappointed in it, like most Palestinians. The Israelis still control the Palestinian Authority, and the Islamic fundamentalists have taken advantage of this failure to secure any worthwhile progress. The latter will always be a tiny minority, but their message is heard in the refugee camps, where they run social care programmes. The missing ingredient is a minimum of justice, some rules to govern the game. But the Israelis control the borders of Gaza and Jericho, and do much to prevent significant Palestinian development. To some, suicide bombings seem the only method of response left when there is no peace and no justice. The Israeli response is to insist on their own right to security, but an unjust and unstable situation cannot last forever. There remains amongst Palestinians, Christian and Muslim, an abiding sense that God is just, and that Israeli oppression cannot survive merely on the power of its military strength. The speaker thinks that the issue will be thrown into ever-sharper relief on the world stage as the international community criticises ever more strongly Israeli intransigence. Many Americans in our party express their own shame at the US government's continuing double dealing in Middle Eastern affairs, and its tendency always to shoot first. As one Presbyterian minister said, "America is an incurably violent society, and if God does not one day bring down his judgement upon it, then God owes an apology to Sodom and Gomorrah!"

Heady stuff for early morning, but we were heading further east today into the West

Bank, and through the Judean desert. The city is surrounded by increasing numbers of new Jewish settlements, but travelling farther down towards Jericho, it is evident that the desert is not an empty waste. Bedouin still make a living on these bare soils, and we passed many encampments with flocks of sheep and goats. Between the fourth and seventh centuries, countless thousands of Christians left the normalities of civilisation to seek solitude in this very desert. In that period when desert monasticism flourished, this was the busy hub of the monastic world. It was a way of taking literally the urge to move on beyond the life of cities and settled community life altogether. Such a radical movement suffered then and since from the charge of escapism, the desire to avoid the messy conflicts and compromises of the world of everyday. There is a paradox here, certainly. These monks came here from far afield to be near the cities of incarnation and redemption, Bethlehem and Jerusalem, and were closely involved with the controversies which racked the church during that period: the exact nature of Christ's humanity. As one of the greatest of them said: "the monk is one who is separated from all and united to all" (Evagrius). Living in the desert, they kept one eye on the city.

Passing the famous sea-level marker on the road down from Jerusalem to Jericho (and, curiously, the Inn of the Good Samaritan!), we stopped to survey the Judean desert hills. At one time this landscape supported hundreds of monasteries. We began a walk to one of those that survive, the monastery of St. George Choziba in the Wadi Qelt. It is situated crazily on the sheer side of a steep wadi, through which water flowed on a concrete aqueduct halfway up the hillside, constructed, we were told, by the Jordanians in the 1960s. The Greek Orthodox monastic orders are all classed as "Guardians of the Tomb"

Above: People make a living on these bare soils.

St Georges Monastry
Wadi Qelt.

Right: *The Monastery of St George Choziba clings to the cliffs of Wadi Qelt.*

(that is, the Church of the Holy Sepulchre), and their monasteries display the sign (taphos). We entered for a refreshing glass of orange juice – hospitality and charity have always been hallmarks of monastic spirituality, seeking to receive guests as Christ would receive them. This was at the heart of all their work and the test of their way of life. Their chapels were very dark, crowded with icons. The buildings are not all old, but they contain some indications of wall paintings from the Byzantine period. Some monks live in community here, some in cells built into the structure, some in caves higher up the cliff, reached by ladders. In one chapel at the end of a cave lies the preserved body of a former abbot (who died as recently as 1960) along with the bones of others killed by Persians in the sixth century. Life here is lived according to an alternative time-frame.

We walked on down the wadi over rough terrain but through quite stunning scenery. At its foot lies the ruins of a very extensive palace, on the outskirts of Jericho, built over the earlier palace in which Herod the Great died – unmourned. Jericho is now an autonomous Palestinian region, and its policemen in their blue uniforms, not to mention the national flags of red, green and black, were everywhere. The town is a very green oasis in a very brown dry setting.

Left: Hospitality and charity are the hallmarks of monastic spirituality.

Photo-camel: Jericho

Right: *Photo-call for camels and customers: Jericho.*

TEL JERICHO

Tel Jericho is a confusing site to the untrained eye, as many archaeologists' trenches have been dug through it. The most astonishing of all the remains is a stone-built tower dated to 8000BC, part of a settlement so old that it is hardly surprising that the Tel now rises seventy feet above street level. Dating, however, is notoriously difficult, and the place has been abandoned for long periods at several times in its history, as well as suffering violent destruction. Most recent scholarship suggests that the site was uninhabited at the end of the thirteenth century BC when Joshua's entry into Canaan took place (although some archaeologists now challenge that dating). Various attempts have been made to explain the biblical accounts concerning Jericho, the most interesting being that Joshua 6 contains the ritual rubrics for a cultic festival at Gilgal, symbolically celebrating the gaining of the land. Whatever the truth of the matter, the literary "strata" or layers in the Bible are in many ways more difficult to interpret than the archaeological strata on the site.

It proved more difficult to leave Jericho than enter it. In this land of inexplicable complications, it is sometimes far more difficult to travel short distances than make longer journeys. People here live so very close together, yet so far apart. Our driver informed us that since we left Jerusalem the West Bank and Jericho had suddenly been closed off. Sure enough, we found a long line of trucks lined up at the border checkpoint, situated on wasteland that had been a refugee camp between 1948 and 1967. All the trucks were laden with fresh produce, now suddenly prevented from getting to market. Tempers were clearly frayed as drivers crowded in the road, complaining noisily. Our coach was allowed to slip to the front of the queue, and two Israeli soldiers with

Below: Palestinian boys race donkeys: Jericho

submachine guns came onto the bus and proceeded to check all our baggage. This took half an hour before we were allowed to proceed. A little further on we stopped to pick up a Palestinian woman. At the next roadblock she was asked to move to the centre of the coach so that the soldiers would not see her! We had a good conversation with this intelligent woman who has worked in a personnel office in Jericho since independence in 1994, but whose husband in Jerusalem has no work. Her family, who for generations have been keepers of the el-Aqsa mosque, never knows each day when, or whether, she will get home. They were forced off their land and home in 1948, to endure poverty ever since.

Below: A stone tower at Jericho that was ancient long before Jesus' time.

Chapter Seventeen

BACK TO THE FUTURE

An Arabic Eucharist at St. George's Cathedral is actually celebrated in English and Arabic, as there are so many European and American pilgrims present. The Arabic-speaking congregation is small, a sign of the diminishing size of the Palestinian Christian population, caught between the two majority traditions. Its position is a critical one, and never more so since the Israeli Defence Force has been in alliance with a Christian faction in southern Lebanon against its Arab neighbours. It tries to maintain some kind of balance between its own Christian identity in the land of Jesus, its commitment to Palestinian nationhood, its somewhat sensitive relations with the Islamic Arab majority, and its reputation as a highly educated Arab elite within a Jewish state system. Life can be spitefully difficult in such a church. The Bishop claims that there is more barbed wire in his diocese than in any other! Many petty restrictions on movement between Israel proper and the occupied territories govern deployment of clergy. Some are Israeli Arabs, some have no formal status. Some have residency permits in Jerusalem, some do not, and these can be summarily withdrawn on the slightest pretext, as the creeping Judaization of Jerusalem gradually surrounds this hemmed-in community.

In the busy crowded neighbourhood, down Salah-e-din Street towards the Damascus Gate, Sunday is the first day of the working week, and business was brisk. The pavements are crowded, while cars, buses, taxis and trucks compete fiercely for the inadequate road space with liberal use of horns and expletives. At the end of the street outside the post office there is always an army presence, young soldiers, each with their automatic rifle, spilling out of the back of jeeps, stopping cars and mounting foot patrols. Occasionally a mounted detachment passes by, the horses' hooves shod with some soft material that prevents their approach being heard. Crossing the road, not as easy as it sounds when pedestrians and vehicles compete for every inch of space, and walking through the Damascus

Gate "Peddlers' Market", is like moving over an invisible line between two communities, East and West. Suddenly there are no *kefiyahs* to be seen, no spoken Arabic overheard, no litter on badly maintained streets, no veiled women, no open stalls selling fresh produce, no aromas of spices and freshly roasted coffee. Instead there is a different world of shop fronts and multi-lane highways.

KEEP YOUR HEAD DOWN

I particularly wanted to find some way of reaching a site I had never previously visited because of disturbances in the West Bank. Most tourist guidebooks warn of the risk, and suggest extra vigilance, or even avoidance. "Keep your head down" was the gist of advice I was offered at St. George's College. But I had seen the prominent flat-topped cone of Herodion on the horizon when we had been in Bethlehem, rather like an extinct volcano. I was determined to get there if I could. Taxi drivers everywhere, it is said, know everything that is happening locally, and will usually talk about it at some length if asked. Monir Khweis was no exception to this rule, except that he did not wait to be asked. We accepted his reasonable price for the round trip, and were treated to an animated Arab Muslim presentation of the current situation as we drove out of the city. His English was sufficiently good to express the passion of his views.

"There are few tourists now, they are frightened to come. There is no peace, and Israelis want no peace, no justice. They are selfish, they teach their children hatred. They think God gave them this land, but we are all God's children, and we should live in peace. Half the Israelis do want peace, but the other half, and the government also, want to stop the peace process and encourage the settlements. Why should I give up my land, my father's

Below: Jewish police horses "parked" on a bus stand in East Jerusalem.

Above: Herodion; where Herod built an elaborate complex — a "monument to megalomania, paranoia and fear".

land and his father's before him, so that these people from all over, from Russia, from everywhere, can come and take it from me? I was a boy in 1948, and my grandfather told me that Jews and Arabs lived together in those days. I have never seen it in my life. But it is all under God. God is punishing the Arab nation because it does not trust God anymore. Everyone wants to be in control. When do you think there will be peace? They have no respect for your British government. Israel is a superpower. They think they can do what they like. America? The Congress is full of Jews. Everyone must have patience, and then God's justice will come. It is just like Moses bringing his people from Egypt. They had to wait because they wanted to do it their way, not God's way. I know the Bible, I read the Koran. We have to be patient. But now the Israelis are doing it again. Yes, so many of them were killed in Europe, but why can't they learn from their own history? There is so much pressure on the Arabs. They are frightened of us. We have been here a long time. The situation will not last. Either it will explode. Or it will be peace. God knows. You must trust God".

As this commentary unfolded, we passed Rachel's tomb on the way to Bethlehem. It has now been totally enclosed within a hideous new solid stone building, and is heavily guarded by Israeli soldiers. Monir pointed out contemptuously that the site is holy to Muslims also, but it would take a great deal of courage for any Muslim not to be intimidated by such a show of force.

We passed into the West Bank easily, as the taxi was Israeli-registered. Weaving through the developments in Bethlehem, now under Palestinian autonomy and gearing up for the expected rush of tourists celebrating the second Christian millennium, we moved back into the Israeli-occupied territory and the quiet rolling hills of Judea, rocky terrain baked brown and dry. Life moves at a much slower pace, though many new housing developments have been started. The grant aid for Palestinian development, however, has not yet got as far as road-building programmes, which are badly needed. Real driving skill is needed to avoid not only the holes on our side of the road but also the oncoming cars likewise avoiding the holes on theirs, not to mention slow-moving flocks of sheep and goats. None of this held up the running commentary on the situation.

The only visitors to the site were three armed soldiers and ourselves. Fully excavated only in recent years, it did nothing to change the view of Herod the Great we had formed elsewhere. It is a monument to megalomania, paranoia and fear. History does tend to repeat itself. Herodion is an immense complex of pools, gardens and annexes for family and officials at the base of the mountain, and a palace within a circular fortress on its summit. When the buildings were standing at their full height, it must have presented an impregnable face to the world. But to walk around its ruins is to realise the futility of such grandiose schemes. Many subsequent occupants – Romans, Jewish rebels, Byzantine monks, Bedouin, and now archaeologists – have put it to a variety of uses, including claims to the territory on which it stands.

BROWN HILLS

A walk round the summit provides incredible views over the surrounding area of brown hills, with the white sprawling town of Bethlehem prominent in the near distance. Small Arab settlements, with their dusty roads and square-built stone houses, dot the landscape. Noticeable by its lusher vegetation and distinctive architecture of evenly spaced houses with sloping red roofs, however, is one of the many Jewish settlements that have sprung up in the West Bank in recent years. We mentioned this in the taxi on our return. In response we were taken back to Jerusalem by a different route so that we could see the bare mountain called Abu Ghneim, or Har Homa as the Israelis call it, now causing international attention as an illegal settlement. It is very close to the Christian Arab communities of Beit Sahur and Bethlehem, and its site could not have been more provocatively chosen. Just here the hillside has already been cut away for a brand new road to serve this planned new Jewish district. It will complete a circle of Jewish settlements around Arab

Left: *Olives for nutrition; oil for light; and a symbol of peace.*

Jerusalem, cutting off Beit Sahur and Bethlehem from the city itself, and the rest of the West Bank. These housing projects are in effect asserting total Jewish control of Jerusalem, in defiance of international agreements and opinion. It fuels the fires of nationalistic hatred, and adds hugely to the nightmarish preoccupation with security.

Monir had clearly suggested to us that Jew and Arab had lived relatively peacefully together in the same land before 1948. Before that, of course, local people had not governed the region; Herod had simply been one in a long line of foreign or puppet rulers. Local Jews and Arabs, both Muslim and Christian, were all of Semitic race, mostly spoke Arabic, and did not instigate the Palestinian problem. Zionism came from Europe. Local Arabs were displaced and dispersed by Jewish people from elsewhere. The resulting argu-

Right: *In the ruins of Herodion.*

ments have since become deeply racial and religious. Zionism has created a new state rooted in racial identity. For this, European Christianity must accept much of the blame (and take the responsibility). Now the Islamic revival has created its own kind of religious fundamentalism. Both Orthodox Jews and fundamentalist Muslims today insist on their God-given rights, rather than international law. The West finds it very difficult to recognise, or deal with, the tragic fact that the Israeli-Palestinian question has regressed to more tribal notions. Secular notions of rational decision, natural justice and equal human rights do not count for very much in the face of assertions that "God gave us this land in perpetuity". Monir had really been speaking of a common faith, rooted in Adam, centred in Abraham. Faith unites, religion divides. And in Jerusalem that is a matter of life and death.

Chapter Eighteen

GOING BY TRAIN

The Rockefeller museum, not far from St. George's Cathedral, is a stately building built during the period of British mandate, and still bears scars from the fighting of 1967. The interior, built around a handsome courtyard, is a reminder of what all British museums used to be like before interactive presentations became the fashion – assorted artefacts displayed in rows of glass cases. Several important items have been moved to the Israel museum in west Jerusalem, but the design of the whole is instructive. Each period in the history (and pre-history) of the Holy Land is assigned one of fourteen bays, from 3000BC until the medieval period. The fact that the period of the Israelite kingdoms is assigned only one such bay helps to put the time of the Old Testament into a historical perspective.

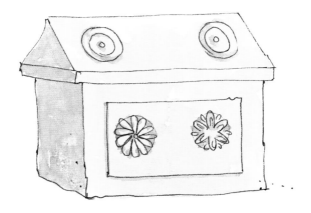

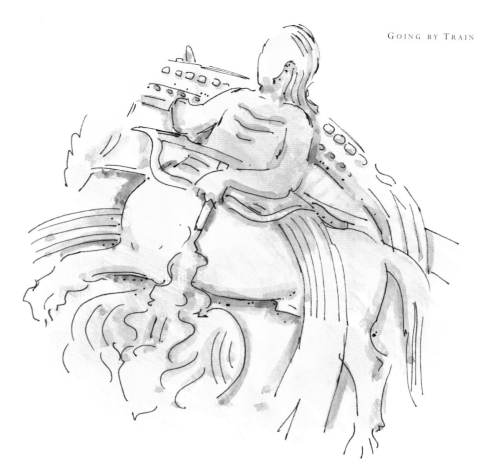

Left: Sagittarius, from the 12th century Crusader.

Pride of place in the museum is given to the pair of twelfth-century carved marble friezes that surmounted the Crusader entrance to the Church of the Resurrection until they were moved here to prevent further erosion in the 1930s. They reveal handsome carving of scenes from the life of Jesus, but also a surprising amount of non-figurative carving – medallions, intertwined branches, flowers, centaurs, cavorting nude youths, a quite surprising use of pagan motifs over the door of a major Christian church!

HINNOM VALLEY

It was such a lovely hot and sunny day, we walked across to the Jaffa gate and through beautifully laid out gardens to the famous King David Hotel. Past the Montefiore windmill and across the Hinnom valley is the railway station. Constructed in 1892 as a narrow gauge railway, it did much to open up Jerusalem's development, doubling its population to 75,000 by 1914. Under the Mandate it was brought up to standard gauge, with routes to Tel Aviv, Haifa, Damascus and Cairo. Alas, travel by rail is not what it was. There is but one train each day to Tel Aviv, and the station looks exactly as it does in old photographs of General Allenby arriving in 1917! The rolling stock is not much newer, an aged diesel locomotive and two rotting carriages that had obviously seen better days on the Deutsches

Bundesbahn, to judge by the underpaintings on the carriage sides. With only a handful of passengers, the train snakes slowly out through the western suburbs, and although it is downhill all the way, takes a full two hours to reach Tel Aviv.

"It requires only an ordinary amount of activity", wrote a passenger on the line in 1901, "to jump out and pick the flowers along the line, and rejoin the train as it laboriously pants up the steep ascent". Nevertheless we are able to appreciate countryside entirely missed by the buses that do the journey in less than half the time on the new sweeping highway. The line is engineered to hug the contours, and winds its way through a very narrow ravine. There is no road through this, the Soreq valley, once the home of Delilah, temptress of Samson. At one point the line runs through what is now the West Bank, at which point two young men in front of us suddenly jumped up, produced concealed sub-machine guns which they pushed out of the windows on either side of the train. Recovering from shock, I noticed high up on the valley side a small Arab village with an Israeli armed platoon guarding our progress. I subsequently learnt that the train was in fact ambushed recently, and no chances are taken. The one nearly-empty train each day is presumably kept open for reasons other than economics. Near journey's end the terrain flattens out, passing large-scale mineral workings before edging through the less salubrious parts of Tel Aviv into a brand-new downtown station crowded with commuters on a fast north-south line to Haifa.

THE THREAT

Looking for the right bus in a large open square packed with people, we suddenly heard a loud report. Half the crowd was immediately lying flat on the road and surrounding grass, such is the instinctive reaction of a people who live under constant threat of bomb attack. A moment's fear, then soldiers and police appeared as if from nowhere, clearing the entire bus station. Every bus was searched, but nothing was found. We were somewhat later than expected arriving back in Jerusalem. Terrible things do happen here occasionally, often on buses.

Hastily hand-written notice in corridor of Rockefellar — a sign of the times.

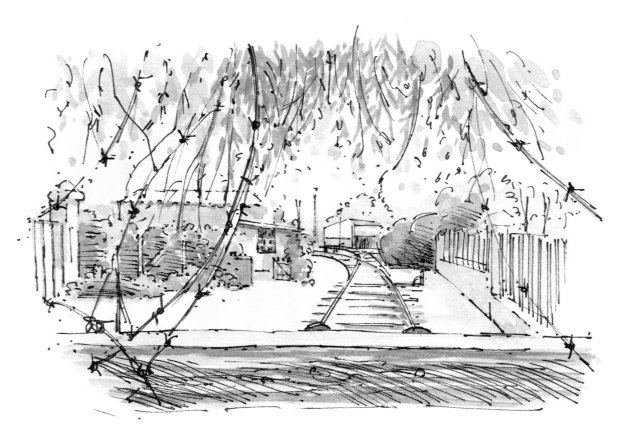

Above: Jerusalem terminus.

Chapter Nineteen

THE JOURNEY —
ONWARDS TO EMMAUS

Today we leave Jerusalem. Only a short distance away is Emmaus, but it is not easy to find! At least four different places have been identified at some period of history as *the* Emmaus. This, partly because various manuscripts of Luke's gospel suggest different distances from the city – 160 stadia, 60 stadia one way, or 60 stadia round trip. The latter seems most likely as within walking distance.

Imwas was first recognised by the early church however as the site farthest from Jerusalem. It occupies a strategic site on the main route to the coast, and until the seventh century was a flourishing city known as Nicopolis. What was left of it was totally destroyed by the Israelis in 1967.

Abu Ghosh, closer to Jerusalem, was chosen by the Crusaders in the twelfth century as the site where they would remember the Emmaus story. Their severe and beautiful church still stands, home to a French Benedictine community. I shall never forget attending the Easter morning plainchant liturgy there on a previous visit.

The Abu Ghosh road became dangerous for Christian pilgrims after the Crusaders left. Qubeibeh, on a safer main route from Jerusalem, had by 1500AD become identified with Emmaus. Latin Christians still gather there for worship every Easter Monday.

The site nearest to Jerusalem is well within the western suburbs of the ever-expanding modern metropolis. Turning off the highway at the Motza interchange, the ruins and rubble of former Palestinian homes are still evident – another Arab village destroyed in 1948. From a narrow street near some newly built Israeli houses, we began walking up a stony track seeming to lead nowhere. A man glanced up as we went by, and called to us over his fence, "Why are you going up there? There's nothing there!" That is how it seemed to us too, but some distance farther up the hill we stumbled across what turned out to be a very large Roman period cistern. Clearly a community of some size had existed here. Looking down at the path we were walking, a considerable stretch of Roman paved road, apparently dating from the Hasmonean period, could be made out under the debris and undergrowth. Soon to be swallowed up, probably, by the housing developments creeping up the still wooded hillside. Motza. The word does sound similar to "Emmaus". There was obviously a sizeable village here, and this was part of the ancient road leading back to Jerusalem! We gathered round to wonder about all this, and someone read the text from Luke 24. The reality of the risen Christ, explicit and obvious in the simple acts of conversation, hospitality and shared food. Did not our hearts burn within us?

Of course, Emmaus is wherever we want it to be, because it is a story about meeting Jesus, and that happens independent of place and circumstance. At Imwas, where armies have struggled and blood has been shed, there exist now small communities of reconciliation. Wherever peoples of separate traditions and different convictions reach out to one another in hope of eventual unity, there is a genuine Emmaus, a meeting with Christ. In Abu Ghosh, or any place where people's hearts and minds are stirred to find God's beauty in the splendour of his creation, the risen Christ meets us. At Qubeibeh, and wherever Christians gather to read the scriptures and break bread together, the risen Christ is present. And at Motza too, where there is nothing to see but desolation and bitter memories. Wherever people suffer, and wherever others stretch out their hands to help them,

Above: Had we found the real Emmaus?

Christ is present. None of these places are necessarily located in Palestine. Emmaus is any-where we make room or time in our lives for the stranger, the other person, the other point of view. We all felt the impact of this story in new ways as we walked back down the hill to the bus, into the setting sun glowing gold in the west, and on towards Tel Aviv and our flight home.

MOVING WESTWARDS

Like us, Luke's narrative also leaves Jerusalem and moves westwards towards Emmaus. What happens there sends the three disciples scurrying back to Jerusalem, only to find that things have moved on, beyond Jerusalem. Why is the account of the walk to Emmaus only found in Luke's gospel? Perhaps because Luke's whole gospel story is a journey. In Luke's second book, the Acts of the Apostles, the story progresses even further west-wards, as far as Rome. Josephus tells the same story of the fall of Jerusalem in his Jewish Wars. Luke's story is a global one, and presented in a way that is central, not marginal, to the world's concerns. It begins in Palestine, but does not stay there. As the world's centre becomes established in Rome, so the focus of Christianity shifts there too. The Christian way passes through Jerusalem. Luke's work has a double structure, of Jesus going up to Jerusalem (in the gospel) and of the Church going away from Jerusalem (in Acts).

It may be that Luke learnt his Christian theology from Paul, writing and travelling dur-ing the very first generation of the Christian era. Paul had sharp disagreements with the Christians in Jerusalem, still tied to old ways. For Paul, the new centre for faith was not any physical location, of city or temple, but the person of Jesus. Luke tells us how Paul headed for Rome as a centre for missionary expansion. But Paul understood the true pres-ence of God in the world to be an indwelling of God's Spirit in the life of people. It was a revolutionary new outlook for which he needed to argue long and hard with his Jewish contemporaries (in his letter to the Romans, for example). For Jewish people, the con-cept of religious life and pilgrimage was of course bound to Jerusalem as the only goal, a concept applied by one early Christian writer to a "heavenly Jerusalem"(Hebrews 12:22).

In John's Gospel, Jesus' long journey from Galilee seems not to play a part in the nar-rative design. There must be a reason for this alternative version of events. John is clearly writing for Palestinian Jews, deeply conscious of the new outlook gaining ground in Jerusalem. The doubters could easily write off Jesus as a marginal Galilean, and John is at pains to stress that Christianity challenges and replaces the fundamental and central prin-ciples of nationalistic Judaism. Jesus is not marginal – he is the new centre. Most scholars in fact think that John had himself already left Palestine behind by the time he came to write his gospel, and that the Temple there had already been destroyed. John's gospel is not about a journey to Jerusalem at all, but rather a new journey outward that he himself had already begun.

So where is the "real" Jerusalem? (The Internet offers tours of virtual Jerusalem). In earlier theologies, it was at the world's foundation and centre. Today it remains at the cen-tre of unresolved conflict and the flashpoint of world peace and religious harmony. In the spiritual traditions of Judaism, Christianity and Islam, it remains the centre of an eternal promised land, but ambiguously so, for all but the most literally fundamentalist of those traditions know that the purposes of God cannot be so constrained. The ancient Jewish longing for Jerusalem has always been for more than territory, and certainly not for the tourist theme park it now threatens to become. One of the greatest medieval Jewish poets, Judah haLevi, voiced it:

Lord, where shall I find you?
Your place is high and concealed.
But where shall I fail to find you?
Every place is your glory revealed.

The cherubim serve as a throne,
Yet you dwell far above every place,
The spheres of the sky are too small,
The Temple defective of space.

To you I have longed to come near,
With you I am yearning to be:
In my quest I found you on the road
Already close searching for me.

For Christian believers, the Jerusalem image became a common poetic synonym for heaven, expressed in countless popular hymns:

Urbs beata Hierusalem *(Blessed city, heavenly Salem)*
sixth century

Chorus novae Hierusalem *(Ye choirs of new Jerusalem)*
eleventh century

Urbs Sion aurea *(Jerusalem the golden)*
BERNARD OF CLUNY twelfth century

Jerusalem luminosa *(Light's abode, celestial Salem)*
THOMAS AQUINAS thirteenth century

Jerusalem my happy home
BASED ON AUGUSTINE sixteenth century

My soul, there is a country
HENRY VAUGHAN seventeenth century

And did those feet in ancient time
WILLIAM BLAKE nineteenth century

It is also a strong liturgical image for what lies beyond this earthly pilgrimage:

"Go forth upon your journey out of the world … may your dwelling be this day in peace … may the angels lead you into paradise; may the martyrs come to welcome you and take you to the holy city, the new and eternal Jerusalem."

We cannot always be moving on, and never staying. We cannot always stay in the same place, and never moving forward. The image of the spiritual journey is an ambiguous one.

The Christian life requires an ability to live in more than one place at once. We must have feet on the ground, committed to the context, community and culture of which we are part, yet also live imaginatively and faithfully in hope, for others perhaps more than ourselves. The places we inhabit in reality are woven together with dreams and hopes of what they might become; it is our faith that gives added value and meaning to our everyday experience. It is the Christian's task to build bridges between these two conditions, reality and hope. The connections must not be too simplistic, as though the perfect world could correspond literally to our mere description, or fantasy, of it. These are the temptations of the religious fundamentalist, the dangers of which are obvious. Nor must the connections be merely the naive projections of the religious enthusiasts, who ignore the claims of the real world in order to go and live in their castles in the air. The challenge is how to live in ways by which the unknown future can yet transform our present existence. The "real presence" – a phrase drawn from eucharistic theology – must not be restricted to the symbol, ignoring the reality thus symbolised.

At the heart of the Emmaus story is just such a eucharist.

Right: Physical sustenance. But we also need spiritual sustenance.

Below: *First century Roman water cistern: Motza.*

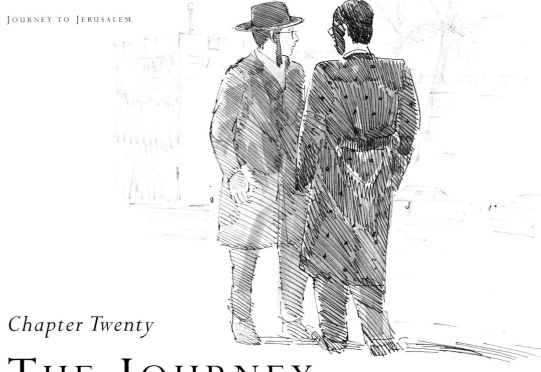

Right: *Living in Jerusalem,
at the crossroads of history
and theology.*

Chapter Twenty

THE JOURNEY
— HOMEWARDS,
INWARDS

It is less than three weeks since we set foot in the Holy Land, and arrived at Ben
Gurion airport. Needless to say, it feels much longer than that. We have made
several long, overlapping journeys.

Security arrangements are such, with good reason, that we arrived at the departure
lounge exhausted after much questioning of where we have been, who we have met, what
we have done, what we are carrying. But even this interrogation, often brusque, is slight
in comparison with the questions we now have to ask ourselves, not about where we have
been, but about where we are going!

Eventually, in the early hours, our plane lifts off into the night, and we all find ourselves
wondering whether we shall ever return to this land. We shall certainly take a great deal
of it home with us. Tourists move through the places they visit. For us, the holy places have
passed through us …

As we fly homewards, I cannot help but recall how literal minds in Jerusalem have
interpreted the end of the gospel story, the story of the ascension of Jesus placed near
Bethany on the Mount of Olives ridge. Images of the prints of departed feet, and representations of Jesus soaring upwards into the sky, badly mistake the nature of this episode,
which is, like all the others, a story of a journey at several levels. It is a kind of recapitu-
lation of the earlier story of the transfiguration. Maybe it is the same story that has somehow become displaced in the narrative, as many scholars think. No matter; the story cer-

tainly bears repeating. The ascension of Jesus is a recognition, first, of the theological status of Jesus. It serves as the conclusion and climax of the whole narrative. The whole
meaning of the gospel, which as we have noticed throughout is implicit in every moment,
is now made explicit. The journey moves on in other ways. The final ascension story indi-
cates the beginning of and the signal for the journey of the new Christian community to
begin and to continue. It is a journey of geographical expansion and intellectual development and spiritual development. In each case it is a journey outward and forwards, crossing national and racial and political and social boundaries. Of course, such a journey
demands also a journey inwards, and homewards. The essence of the whole story of Jesus
is surely that this Jesus is available to every people, and is no longer restricted to a troublesome race in a troublesome corner of an ancient empire. People do not need to make
expensive pilgrimages to the shrines where events in his life may or may not have taken
place. This is the paradox with which we began. None of us regret making this journey. It
has been the chance to study the text of the gospel more deeply in its own context. It has
come alive in new ways. And the question is whether we too will come alive in new ways
as a result.

IN THE HOLY LAND WITH A BIBLE

The long flight allows me to turn to the bible readings for the day. This journey in the Holy
Land with a Bible will have a lasting effect on the way I study the Bible in the future, wherever I happen to be. I turn to Zephaniah 3, an exultant expression of faith in the restoration of Jerusalem, and cannot help remembering, with sadness, what we saw and heard
there during the past few days. We sensed how the longings of many different peoples are
bound up with the history and future of that city. Jerusalem still stands at the heart of
God's work on earth. Those ancient maps with Jerusalem at the world's centre are true
theological maps. Zephaniah too places it at the heart of God's purpose for every city and
every community. About two and a half millennia ago, he envisages God's people holding
a carnival there. Christian living too is a carnival — it is about hope and promise, not
cynicism and despair, despite appearances.

The other reading for the day is in Mark 2. Jesus comes home, and huge crowds gather outside his house. The only way four men can bring their paralysed friend to Jesus is to
break open the roof! My mind returns at once to that sunny day among the houses and
grinding stones of Capernaum. But I remember too that through his encounters with the
broken human condition in the towns and villages of Galilee, Jesus was responding to the
sharpest issues of his own time. Theology will always bring controversy, because we are
called to live and share the breaking in of God's rule, and the kingdom of God is always
pitted against alternative orders.

I reflect that I could turn now to almost any biblical passage and see how it would point
back home, and to the task of preparing for Christian ministry *in our own reality*. This biblical journey has been overloaded, saturated, leaving far too much to absorb. We have tried
to make the most of our opportunities. Now we need time to reflect, to let it sink in so
that it can be truly part of us. The experience of being in the biblical places must become
real in our own places, it must be woven through our memories, our photographs, our

conversations, our prayers, our bible study, so that our hearts go on burning within us… When we return, and people ask: "How was it?" we shall need to articulate what we have learned, through hard listening, sweaty walks, physical endurance and personal struggle, through things we didn't expect. We shall remember how things drop into place unexpectedly. We shall need to recall how the Bible makes a different kind of sense when we read it in its own very real context.

A WAY OF LIFE

The practice of Christianity is often described as a way of life, a way of following Jesus, and therefore a way to God. What we have discovered is that all Christian living is profoundly marked by the hallmarks of Jesus' own journey, a journey out, back and inwards, through exile, exodus and sacrifice. As we moved through the biblical lands, we noticed how deeply the biblical stories were rooted in their actual contexts, and how the telling of the stories provided the resources for each subsequent generation to interact with newer contexts. We noticed how inescapably real and historical those stories are, embedded in the actual events of ordinary people, and yet told in such a way that they lead beyond the mundane to the heart of all religious commitment in the true nature of sacrifice. So the journey of Jesus, and our journey with Jesus, is not so much a way to God, as a journey with God.

We have tried during these weeks to see Jesus more clearly by concentrating on his actual background, his milieu, the Jewish and Greek worlds in which he lived, the long biblical story of which he was part. We have come much closer to Jesus as a real historical person, and we have understood a little more clearly how subsequent generations of his followers up to and including our own have interpreted him for their own needs, their own times and places. This will be the work of our continuing journey, seeking to understand our own faith and practice in following this man, against the very different background and culture of our own time and place. We return there, confident in the faith of resurrection, which assures us that Jesus is not confined to the ancient roads of Roman Palestine, but can be just as disconcerting a companion for our journeys too.